# NANTUCKET SOUND

W9-CCN-882

# NANTUCKET SOUND

## A Maritime History

Theresa Mitchell Barbo

THE
History
PRESS

Published by The History Press
Charleston, SC 29403
www.historypress.net

Copyright © 2009 by Theresa Mitchell Barbo
All rights reserved

Front and back cover paintings by William R. Davis, courtesy of Susan and DeWitt
Davenport, Bass River. Back cover photo courtesy of Osterville Historical Society. The
map of Nantucket Sound that appears on the front and back cover is courtesy of the
Normal B. Leventhal Map Center at the Boston Public Library.

First published 2009
Second printing 2010
Manufactured in the United States

ISBN 978.1.59629.687.9

Library of Congress Cataloging-in-Publication Data

Barbo, Theresa M.
Nantucket Sound : a maritime history / Theresa Mitchell Barbo.
p. cm.
Includes bibliographical references and index.
ISBN 978-1-59629-687-9 (alk. paper)
1. Nantucket Sound Region (Mass.)--History, Local. 2. Nantucket Sound Region
(Mass.)--Description and travel. 3. Coasts--Massachusetts--Nantucket Sound. 4. Cape
Cod (Mass.)--History, Local. 5. Martha's Vineyard (Mass.)--History, Local. 6. Nantucket
Island (Mass.)--History, Local. I. Title.
F72.N34.B37 2009
974.4'9--dc22
2009026278

*Notice*: The information in this book is true and complete to the best of our knowledge. It
is offered without guarantee on the part of the author or The History Press. The author
and The History Press disclaim all liability in connection with the use of this book.
All rights reserved. No part of this book may be reproduced or transmitted in any form
whatsoever without prior written permission from the publisher except in the case of
brief quotations embodied in critical articles and reviews.

*To my son, Thomas*
*"My basic principle is that you don't make decisions because they are easy; you don't make them because they are cheap; you don't make them because they're popular; you make them because they're right."*
*—Theodore Hesburgh, University of Notre Dame*

*"Do not go where the path may lead, go instead where there is no path and leave a trail."*
*—Ralph Waldo Emerson*

*And to the memory of my maternal grandmother,*
*Josephine Linarello Ferraro,*
*who perished aboard the Italian liner* Andrea Doria
*south of Nantucket Sound*
*—July 25, 1956.*

*And with much love for Josephine's two daughters,*
*my mother, Clara Ferraro Mitchell,*
*and my dear aunt, Theresa Ferraro Caruso.*

# CONTENTS

# FOREWORD

Nantucket Sound is many things to many people. For the visiting tourists, it's the body of water they travel over on the way to Nantucket or the Vineyard. For fishermen, it's where they work. It has been a source of local food and income for generations of draggermen, charter boats and weir fishermen. The arrival of species like the striped bass and squid will instantly draw hundreds to the Sound.

For those who live on the Cape and Islands, Nantucket Sound is a refuge with wilderness-like views over a landscape unmarred by man. It boasts splendid views, and during the summer it's where local residents escape from tourists.

As land on the Cape and Islands became developed, the shore and waters of Nantucket Sound have been the focus of intense conservation debates for more than forty years. The most notable of these took place in the 1960s, when the Cape Cod National Seashore was established. Back then, there were some who felt that much of the Cape and surrounding waters ought to be added to the park system before it was too late. But any plans to include anything but the Lower Cape were considered politically suicidal. Any ideas of extending the protective umbrella of the federal government were abandoned, at least for the moment.

The next burst of conservation interest came during the 1970s, when energy companies were looking for places to drill for oil. Even though the Sound was of little interest, the widespread fear of a handful of drilling rigs blighting the landscape and threatening the fragile waters prompted state and local officials to create the Cape and Islands Ocean Sanctuary, designating all of Nantucket Sound a protected area. The sanctuary statute noted that Nantucket Sound's rich environment and scenic values were considered worthy of long-term protection and conservation.

Soon after the state created the ocean sanctuary, Congressman Gerry Studds and Senator Edward M. Kennedy filed legislation—endorsed by the entire delegation—to create an Islands Trust. That plan was envisioned as needed to protect the land and waters of the Vineyard and Nantucket and to require the federal government to promote the long-term conservation of the area. While the goals of the legislative proposal had significant support, the specific details of the plan faced mixed reviews. However, the debate alone inspired a number of local conservation efforts, including the creation of regional land use regulatory agencies and land banks to acquire conservation land on both Nantucket and Martha's Vineyard.

In the 1980s, as the federal government started designating a network of national marine sanctuaries, the Commonwealth of Massachusetts made Nantucket Sound its priority. The Nantucket Sound National Marine Sanctuary application filed by the governor and his administration stated:

> *Nantucket Sound contains distinctive ecological, recreational, historic and aesthetic resources that form the basis of the predominant economic pursuits of the area: fishing and tourism. Nantucket Sound is an important habitat containing spawning, nursery and feeding grounds and migration routes for a number of the nation's important living animal resources, an area with high biological productivity and diversity of species, and a premier marine-oriented recreational and historic area of regional and national significance.*

Back then there was no dispute over how the waters of the Sound were to be managed and protected. The debate was usually over who would do it. The state insisted that Nantucket Sound deserved the highest levels of protection, like the Cape Cod National Seashore. The state's management plan included a ban on all forms of power generation, sand and gravel mining and the discharge of any marine wastes. However, the state proposed a unique system of management that would bring together state, local and federal systems into one overall and coordinated effort. Even though it would be a national sanctuary, the state would take the lead in the effort.

The Massachusetts plan was quite similar to the marine sanctuary established in the Florida Keys, where state and federal natural resources management staff and officials work under one overall management plan and one overall umbrella organization. The Florida plan also established a fund to provide federal dollars to pay for sewer projects and other measures to protect the coastal waters of the Florida Keys. The Massachusetts and Florida plans were "ecosystem based," visionary and well ahead of their time.

The Nantucket Sound Sanctuary proposal was endorsed by an independent panel of scientists, the National Oceanographic and Atmospheric Administration and the United States Fish and Wildlife Service. The campaign to make Nantucket Sound a National Marine Sanctuary was precipitated, in part, by the anticipated outcome of a Supreme Court case, *U.S. v. Maine*, which involved coastal boundary disputes involving several states.

State officials, however, were worried about losing control of the middle portion of Nantucket Sound—called the "donut hole"—which was fully protected under the state's own ocean sanctuary statutes. The fear at the time was that a donut hole in the middle of Nantucket Sound would be exposed to weak federal controls. By the time the Supreme Court ruled in 1986 in favor of federal control over the middle of the Sound, the political climate on designating a new sanctuary to protect the area changed significantly. By then, Stellwagen Bank had also emerged as a candidate site worthy of national protection.

Politically, the sanctuary program was popular in Massachusetts, but it came under attack in Washington. Most observers suggested that Massachusetts would only get one sanctuary. Since Stellwagen Bank did not involve multiple political jurisdictions and had an active grass-roots campaign pushing it, that one moved forward. The Nantucket Sound plan was put on the back burner.

Today, plans for wind farms and sand mining for beach nourishment have provoked renewed interest in the long-term protection and conservation of Nantucket Sound. But regardless of the fate of these proposals, new ones will certainly follow. The ocean is getting crowded, and Nantucket Sound is no exception.

The question we must ask ourselves is do we continue to leave the decisions regarding the future of Nantucket Sound to agencies based in Boston and Washington or do we try—once again—to control our own destiny and take matters into our own hands? Before we once again engage in this discussion about how best to protect Nantucket Sound, let us revisit and try to learn from history.

Those of us who love Nantucket Sound and see the need for the long-term protection of the area will cherish Theresa Barbo's book. By looking at the history of Nantucket Sound from the sea, we gain a unique perspective on the history of the area. Barbo brings to life, with a special insight, the rich and vibrant maritime heritage of this area. We learn from this wonderful book that Nantucket Sound has been special for generations.

Today, it is our obligation to protect the Sound—and keep it special—for future generations.

Congressman Bill Delahunt
10th District of Massachusetts

# PREFACE

To my knowledge, this is the first book on Nantucket Sound, though Cape Cod, Martha's Vineyard and Nantucket have inspired hundreds of books by hundreds of authors over hundreds of years. In most of those books, Nantucket Sound merited passing mention, playing only a minor role as quiet understudy. It has been my long-term goal, however, to craft an overview of Nantucket Sound, with the ecosystem and its heritage on center stage as the main character.

While this book is not a cultural history of Martha's Vineyard, Nantucket or Cape Cod, I have included events related to the founding years of English settlements on Nantucket Sound. Simply, and mostly, my goal is to inform, enrich, entertain and extend to a reader a sense of place and uniqueness, value and meaning, of Nantucket Sound.

The maritime and cultural history of Nantucket Sound merits a multi-volume set of books, and it was very difficult determining the cutoff point of what to include and what my editorial "word budget" would allow; I recognize that each person who has sailed through Nantucket Sound had a story, whether it was in 1602 or 2002. Every historical event, through peacetime and war, is an element of the compelling heritage of this historic ecosystem.

I wrestled with format. Halfway through the draft, I ditched the original table of contents that outlined Nantucket Sound's cultural and maritime history in venerable chronological order. After composing began, it became clear that combining themes of lightships and lighthouses, or fishing and whaling, for example, seemed logical and flowed well. Clusters of subject matter dictated order of content but a timeline still existed, so I don't regret switching gears on lark and gut instinct. Throughout the draft, I left intact verbatim passages and quotes of historical figures despite awful grammar

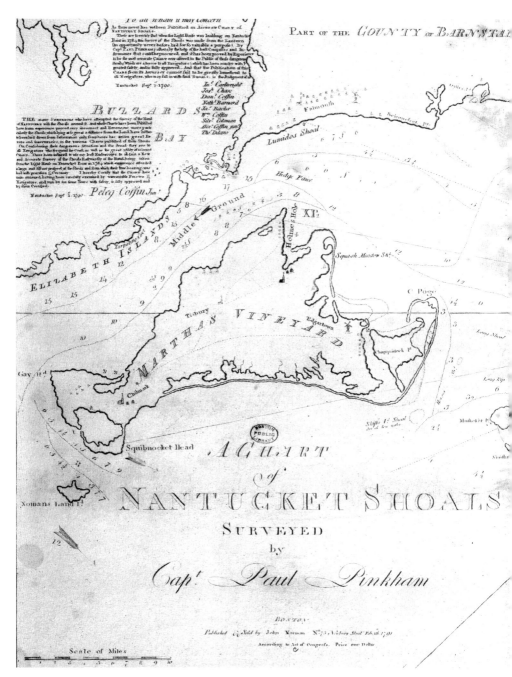

By 1794, mapmaking had evolved into a sophisticated science, as evidenced by the work of Captain Paul Pinkham. *Courtesy of the Norman B. Leventhal Map Center, Boston Public Library.*

Sails raised and racing in Nantucket Sound. *Painting by William R. Davis. Courtesy of Susan and DeWitt Davenport, Bass River.*

and spelling; I believe authentic words define for the reader the truth of past ages and the raw grit of previous cultures. The authenticity of these quotes humanizes each era.

I hope you will share in my respect and regard for this ecosystem once you've finished the book. The bibliography spans hundreds of years, reflecting sociological trends, attitudes and beliefs of the authors, many of whom were historical figures; from a research vantage, seeing these beliefs and attitudes evolve was compelling for me.

I am not Cape Cod born and bred, and the Sound is a long way from the woods of northern Indiana where I came of age along the banks of the St. Joseph River in South Bend. Salt views, therefore, I never take for granted and the seascape ages never; I've lost count of the times I've stood at the shores of Nantucket Sound, staring into the seas, searching for everything but seeing nothing in particular. Even during storms I see only its lee side. I have never outgrown the sense of awe of Nantucket Sound, and I hope I never will.

# ACKNOWLEDGEMENTS

Few works of historical nonfiction are solo ventures. Many smart, kind people assisted with this book. I am grateful to Mary Sicchio of the William Brewster Nickerson Room at Cape Cod Community College and Falmouth Historical Society for her guidance and good cheer. Cynthia D. Hall, executive director of the Osterville Historical Museum; Desiree Mobed, executive director of the Harwich Historical Society; Maureen Rukstalis of the Historical Society of Old Yarmouth; Marcella Curry, deputy director of Sturgis Library in Barnstable; and Karen Horn, also at Sturgis, were always helpful. Marie Henke and Elizabeth Oldham at the Nantucket Historical Association, and Keith Gorman at the Martha's Vineyard Museum, were helpful during site visits earlier this spring. Burt Derick and Phyllis Horton of the Dennis Historical Society and John Roche of Harwich provided insightful information. Others who contributed time, efforts, advice and good cheer include Jeremy King and Vincent Malkoskie at the Massachusetts Department of Marine Fisheries and staff at the Nathan B. Levanthal Map Center at Boston Public Library, including Curator Ronald E. Grim and Angela Bonds, the cartographic technician.

Composers of appendices were Gil Newton of Sandwich High School and Cape Cod Community College, William Burke of the Cape Cod National Seashore and Lisa Berry-Engler of the Massachusetts Coastal Zone Management Office in Boston. I urge you to read their work; these appendices greatly complement understanding about Nantucket Sound. Tanya Grady helped locate several scholarly articles, and my neighbor, Ralph Alberti, shared past issues of *Maritime Life and Traditions*. William R. Davis, the renowned maritime artist, painted the beautiful artwork you see on the cover and back of the book and inside its pages, and I am grateful to Susan and DeWitt Davenport of Bass River, who allowed the use of their paintings from their private collection in this book. Captains Douglas K. and Linda J. Lee of Rockland, Maine, shared the image of the doomed schooner *Wyoming*, and Gordon Massingham, owner of Detrick Lawrence Productions on Martha's Vineyard, generously shared his images of Zeb Tilton and other pictures. I am grateful for the extra sets of eyes of colleagues who read the manuscript draft and greatly improved the content: Lee Ferguson Gruzen, Gordon Massingham, Mary Sicchio, James J. Coogan Jr., Maurice Gibbs, Burton Nickerson Derick, Heather Rockwell, Richard Ryder, Linda Coombs, Phyllis Horton and William Collette. My thanks to Bob Dwyer, executive director of the Cape Cod Museum of Natural History, who offered the use of the Hay Library there, where much of the draft was composed, and to fellow scribe Russ Webster for his contribution and support. Two experienced boatmen are owed thanks: Terry Clen and Steve McKenna, with whom I traveled atop the Sound during the research phase of this book.

The team at The History Press is second to none. Senior commissioning editor and publisher J. Saunders Robinson, to whom I'm most grateful for yet another wonderful collaboration, deserves thanks, along with Hilary McCullough, Julie Foster, Brittain Phillips, Lara Simpson, Dani McGrath and Marshall Hudson.

My gratitude to Congressman Bill Delahunt, who composed the Foreword, especially to Chief of Staff Mark Forest. Special gratitude to my family: my husband, Dan, and our children, Katherine and Thomas.

# Chapter One

# CONTEXT

*Change is the only constant.*
*—Heraclitus*

*The three great elemental sounds in nature are the sound of rain, the sound of wind in a primeval wood, and the sound of outer ocean on a beach.*
*—Henry Beston*

Nantucket Sound is smaller than boundaries often envisioned, though approximately six hundred square miles of water are indeed relative. Nantucket Sound—about thirty miles long and just over twenty-five miles wide—extends from Woods Hole in Falmouth south to West Chop and East Chop on Martha's Vineyard; east to Muskeget and Tuckernuck Islands and the north side of Nantucket; due north toward Monomoy at the extreme eastern end of Chatham and then west through southern Cape Cod towns, beginning at Stage Harbor in Chatham and journeying west to Harwich, Dennis, Yarmouth, Barnstable and Mashpee and back to Falmouth's village of Woods Hole.

Nantucket Sound is a marine basin lined with shoals and rips—extra shallow bars—and is extremely shallow, and therein lays the consistent danger and threat to commercial marine traffic, beginning in the seventeenth century through the present. "There's a good several hundred wrecks, easily, clustered at the entrances to the Sound, either at Monomoy or toward Vineyard Haven," explained Victor Mastone director of the Board of Underwater Archaeological Resources for the Commonwealth of Massachusetts.[1] "Plus there were all these safe harbors and captains had a place to run to" in case of bad weather.[2]

A lone ship at anchor at twilight. *Painting by William R. Davis. Courtesy of Susan and DeWitt Davenport, Bass River.*

Buried beneath sands of the Sound are vessels wrecked on the notorious shallow bars. "We're looking for several wrecks" on the Sound these days, Mastone adds, and he's been surveying the area for several years.[3]

Off Edgartown, the *G.W. Rawley* sank in 1898, and the schooner *Willow* went down in the same area in 1854. Also in their graves in the Sound are the schooners *Sagamore*, which wrecked in 1907, and *Julia A. Rich*, which met the same fate in 1857. There are hundreds more, including the famous six-masted vessel the *Wyoming*.

The Sound was critical to American shipping during the wooden boat era, and it remains a well-traveled highway, minus maintenance headaches of tar, concrete and bridges. Large wooden Boston schooners, according to historian Barry Homer, sailed through Pollock Rip on the extreme eastern edge of the Sound past the tip of Monomoy to Handkerchief Shoals and past the Cross Rip to Vineyard Sound to bypass the shoals to the south of Nantucket. "Sailing through the Sound was almost like threading a needle," Homer said.[4]

I am fortunate to take a short journey on Nantucket Sound with Dennis harbor master Terry Clen, a no-nonsense former Marine and New York Harbor tugboat captain. Clen turns the key on a town-owned Boston whaler docked on the Dennis side of Bass River and we begin a slow run south toward the mouth of Nantucket Sound.

With six masts, the schooner *Wyoming* was the largest schooner ever built. It foundered east of the Pollock Rip in March 1924, sinking with the loss of fourteen crewmen. *Courtesy of Captains Douglas K. and Linda J. Lee.*

Along the way we see a few boats—small skiffs and larger powerboats—moored or docked, waiting for warmer weather and the start of boating season, but hardly a season's complement to the Bass River residential fleet. Clen is an excellent guide: to our east we pass the empty "boater's beach," which on any sunny July weekend, he says, boasts upward of sixty vessels. He's all about safety and openly worries about lack of training of recreational boaters. "You need a license to catch a fish but no license to take twelve people out in a boat," he wryly notes. Still, no doubt boater's beach is safer than the open Sound.[5]

It's chilly, with opaque gray skies and intermittent blue against slight white foam migrating toward shore. Overhead, gulls and seabirds zoom and dart. Indeed, the Sound has always been a birder's paradise and runs along the North Atlantic flyway. Nantucket Sound is a breeding ground for the endangered and federally protected piping plover.

We head into the Sound, where the prevailing southwest winds kick up to at least six knots, and we're bouncing around. Typically, Clen says, winds in the Sound average eighteen knots where it's "rarely flat calm."[6]

Dennis harbor master Terry Clen en route to Nantucket Sound from Bass River. *Photo by Theresa M. Barbo.*

Depending on the slant of the fickle sun, the Sound's color ranges from olive drab to faded jade. Feeling a healthy breeze and smelling salt air are inspiring. To our right is the "rock pile," a small island where nothing grows, but in the nineteenth century packet ships unloaded and smaller vessels bore cargo and passengers to piers up and down Bass River. We are a mile offshore in two feet of water in this section of Nantucket Sound, and the water column is clear and reveals a shell-lined bottom upon a carpet of beige sand and cobbled silt. The silt, sand and cobbles beneath the boat bear silent witness to hundreds of years of natural evolution on Nantucket Sound.

Nantucket Sound was formed by the receding Wisconsin stage of the Laurentian glacier almost twelve thousand years ago.[7] At the glacier's boundary, melting ice deposited moraines, for which scientists have developed three classifications: lateral, median and terminal. These materials are scientific clues and pieces to a geologic formula that's left Nantucket Sound with a mixture of coarse and fine clay and sand with little stratification.[8] Cobbles, pebbles, boulder clay, soft grains of sand and huge boulders line the bottom of Nantucket Sound.[9] Indeed, all of Cape Cod, much of Long Island and north toward Plymouth County are part of what was once a great shelf formed by the receding glacier and melted by streams beneath the unstable debris.[10] Its waters flow to the west at ebb tide and at flood tide to the east.[11]

Nantucket Sound was once a landmass.[12] Indeed, all of southern New England rose at least six hundred feet above what it is today, caused by the uplift of the receding glacier.[13] Until about 9,500 years ago, Nantucket Sound was a lake and the sea level was thirty meters below its present level.[14] Unlike in Cape Cod Bay, the tides in Nantucket Sound range to about three feet. Beneath the sand, the occasional boulder, gravel, cobbles and silt is crystalline basement rock, similar to the rest of the North American continental plate.[15]

The Sound sits at the juncture where cold Labrador currents meet the warm Gulf Stream.[16] Nantucket Sound is part of the larger Nantucket Shelf Region where its southeastern boundary drops into underwater canyons with names such as Atlantis and Munson. Once Georges Bank was above ground until retreating, melting glaciers disappeared at the end of the last ice age and allowed seawater to fill the gaps, reshaping this end of the earth. Inside this approximate five-thousand-square-mile region is Georges Bank, the Great South Channel, the continental shelf south of Martha's Vineyard, Nantucket Shoals, Nantucket Sound and Vineyard Sound.[17] It's an unbelievably huge area.

Today, hook and line fishing is done offshore and outside the Sound within the Nantucket Shelf Region, though a small hook and line fishery remains active in Nantucket Sound. Targeted species include scup and black sea bass, striped bass, bluefish, squid, fluke and tautog, according to the Cape Cod Commercial Hook Fishermen's Association. "The association includes a spectrum of other gear types and fishermen, including weir fishers, pot fishers, shellfishers and commercial bass fishers that do depend on Nantucket Sound and the clean water and good fisheries habitat that it provides," related Susan Nickerson, the "Hook's" executive director.[18] Nickerson is also the Nantucket Soundkeeper, one of many Keepers across the country and overseas that belong to the larger Waterkeeper Alliance, a renowned nonprofit begun by Robert F. Kennedy Jr. "Depending on the target species, the busy season ranges from spring into summer and can continue into the fall. Underscoring the value of the Sound is the fact that it serves as an Essential Fish Habitat for over a dozen species of commercially harvested fish as well as mackerel, butterfish, black sea bass and summer flounder," Nickerson clarified.[19]

Since it began annual research cruises in Nantucket Sound in 1978, the Massachusetts Division of Marine Fisheries has reported over one hundred species of fish and invertebrates that have been "captured, weighed and measured in Nantucket Sound."[20] Two major herring runs are in Harwich and Barnstable, and others are in Dennis and Yarmouth. In truth, commercial and recreational fishing has been the consistent human activity for over four hundred years by English settlers and, before recorded history, Native Americans.

Several centuries ago, right whales were hunted due east of Nantucket, but don't expect to find any large baleen whales in the shallow Sound. Heather Rockwell, who's on the board of Cetacean Society International, wears another hat as the program director for Nantucket Soundkeeper and explains, "We have plenty of toothed whales in the Sound."[21] Rockwell says, "We know this mainly from stranding records and fisheries observations, as there are no dedicated whale watch vessels in the Sound (for good reason); pilot whales, striped dolphins, Atlantic white-sided dolphins, Risso's dolphins, false killer whales and harbor porpoises have all been seen in the Sound."[22] The Sound doesn't have the high concentrations of food resources such as animal plankton—copepods—that right whales prefer; that food source is plentiful from January through May in Cape Cod Bay.[23]

Sharing the corridors are professional and recreational fishermen, merchant mariners and pleasure boaters, scuba divers and water skiers, swimmers, kayakers and sailors. "The bays, coves, inlets and rivers that shape Nantucket Sound's coastline are embedded in my memory, not only for their beauty but for the safe havens they provide," says Lee Gruzen, a writer who grew up in Osterville.[24] "A wonderful variety of boats, moored, docked and launched in these havens, spill out into the open water and crisscross each other in a colorful and mesmerizing display."[25]

Storm systems affect the Sound without mercy. On September 21, 1938, a hurricane rolled up the Atlantic seaboard toward Nantucket Sound and Cape Cod but was particularly harsh on Buzzards and Narragansett Bays. It slammed ashore at high tide around mid-afternoon, producing a surge at least fifteen feet in height and winds upward of 180 miles an hour. In New England, over five hundred people were killed and hundreds more were injured and left homeless. Hundreds of boats moored in inlets and coves in Nantucket Sound were destroyed. Another hurricane on September 14, 1944, hit Cape Cod with winds in excess of 100 miles per hour. Power lines were down and towering trees were ripped up by their roots. Hundreds of homes and buildings were destroyed and damaged, and dozens of people were killed.[26]

Nantucket Sound was designated a state ocean sanctuary in 1970. Another way of quantifying protective measures of the nation's marine resources is through ecosystem-based management, allowing decision makers, resource

The infamous 1944 hurricane lifted boats off moorings and onto the beach off Hyannis. *Courtesy of the Historical Society of Old Yarmouth.*

managers and policy experts to assess what's best for respective waters where the obsolete model of "one size fits all" no longer applies.

In 2008, the Massachusetts Oceans Act, shepherded and sponsored by Cape and Islands state senator Robert O'Leary, updated and reformed measures for science-based policies of protections for waters in the Commonwealth. Unlike, say, Cape Cod Bay, which is all state waters, Nantucket Sound is a mix of local, state and federal jurisdictions, and some areas are under federal protection. The Sound's eastern boundary is joined at the hip to the Monomoy National Wildlife Refuge and Wilderness Area and, farther west, another federal facility, the Waquoit Bay National Estuarine Research Reserve, and Mashpee's National Wildlife Refuge.

Susan Nickerson, the executive director of the Cape Cod Commercial Hook Fishermen's Association, is an avid sailor as well as a Tufts University–trained scientist and policy expert. She has spent hours on the Sound as both a private citizen and Nantucket Soundkeeper to safeguard the Sound's health.

> *Nantucket Sound is the only waterway in the continental U.S. where a large area of federal ocean is surrounded by waters under state jurisdiction. This creates a tremendous management challenge coordinating state and federal interests in a way that protects the Nantucket Sound ecosystem.*

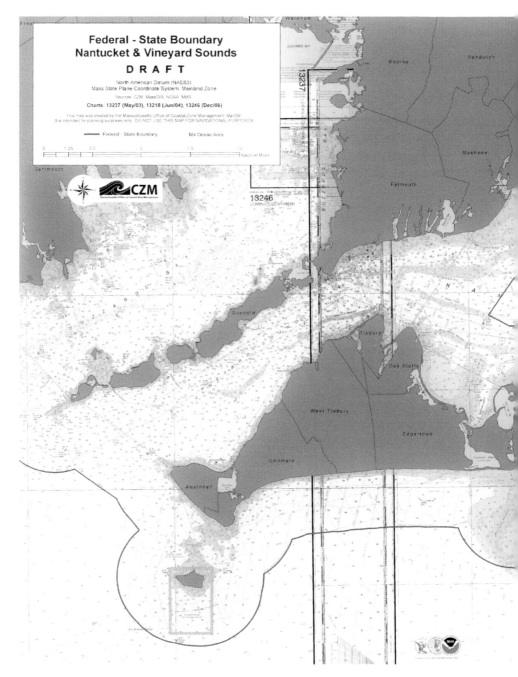

A close-up of state and federal waters in Nantucket Sound. *Courtesy of Massachusetts Coastal Zone Management.*

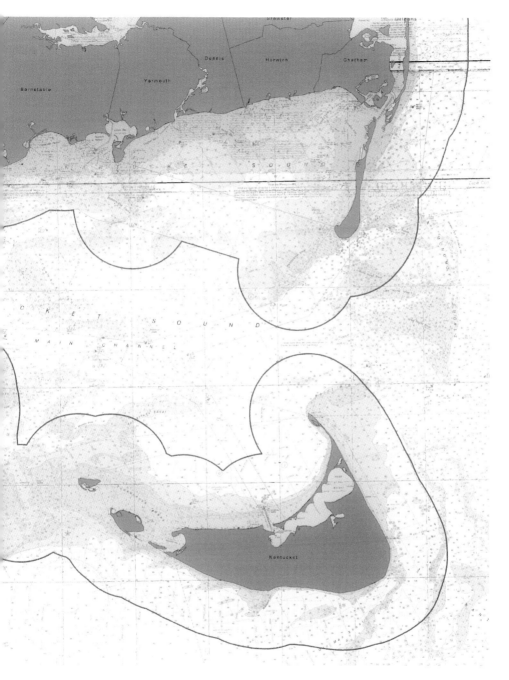

Nantucket Sound is one of five state ocean sanctuaries protected by state law in waters three miles from shore. Federal waters exist in the Sound's middle. *Courtesy of Massachusetts Coastal Zone Management.*

A harvest of clams awaits offloading at Nantucket. *Courtesy of the Nantucket Historical Association.*

> *But the vital role the Sound plays in the ecological richness of our offshore ocean waters, and the value it adds to our social and economic interests on Cape Cod and the Islands, warrants a very high level of protection for all of Nantucket Sound.*[27]

This region of shallow shoals is a wondrous nursery for avian and marine mammal life. Beneath the water sheet, along the stairs of the water column, marine life breeds, lives and dies, from microscopic plankton to schools of fish to whales, all swimming, burrowing, migrating, mating and thriving above the bones of hundreds of wrecked wooden ships. Gray seals breed in the Sound, especially off Monomoy to the east. A squid fishery thrives in the spring. Scallop and other shellfish beds yield an annual bounty, as they have for hundreds of years.

Looking through the lens of a policy analyst or that of a coastal ecologist, Nantucket Sound is a barrier beach-bay system composed of nearly every microsystem in contemporary lexicons: upland areas, freshwater wetlands, rivers and streams, nearshore waters, estuaries and bays, tidal wetlands, embayed islands and brackish/salt ponds. It's a "geoscape" or, plainly, the stuff of inspired poetry and literature.

Nantucket Sound has become accustomed to many roles as an ancient fishing ground of resourceful Native Americans; battleground between

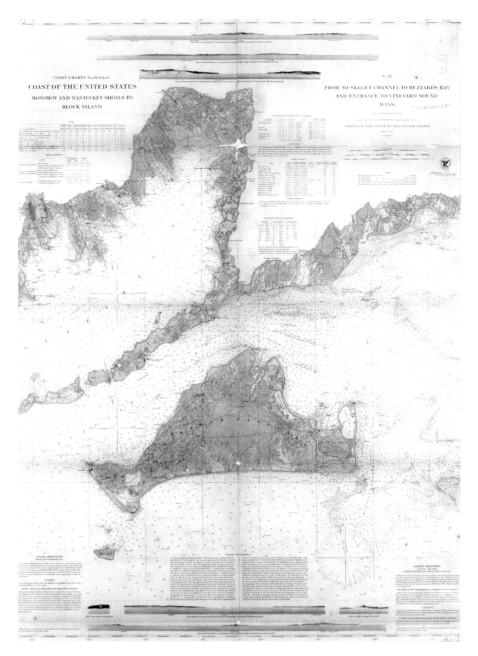

Countless lives and property, including ships, were saved by mariners using Coast Survey maps in Nantucket Sound, such as this guide from 1860. *Courtesy of the Norman B. Leventhal Map Center, Boston Public Library.*

Americans and the British; present-day recreational area and commercial fishing ground; public trust resource; and major marine traffic route in the Northeast.

In the nineteenth century, there existed a degree of sophistication in which science meshed with observation, all to aid mariners. The seminal 1865 *Practical Navigator* by Nathaniel Bowditch deftly and correctly noted conditions in the Gulf Stream: "The warm water of the Gulf Stream is of very different depths at different points of its course, and in different parts of any one of the sections across it. From the deepest portion in the cross sections the warmer water flows off towards the shore, and outwards, overlying the cold."[28]

Before recorded history, Nantucket Sound was the soul of the Native Americans who had fished its waters for thousands of years and made their lives along its shores.

# Chapter Two

# NATIVES AND NEWCOMERS

*We have the right to be what we were created as.*
—*Linda Coombs, Wampanoag Indigenous Programs, Plimoth Plantation*

During summer and fall on Capawack 407 years ago, under a green canopy of dense forest, mostly cedar, oak, elm and beech, inland off the shores of Nantucket Sound, Wampanoag women and girls gathered wild blueberries, cranberries and grapes in reed baskets, communicating in their language, which is part of the Algonquian language family. In their seasonal villages, clay pots simmered over small fires, filled with corn and beans, and often game or fish were added to stew. Against the azure horizon, Wampanoag men and boys hunted for ducks and geese in sheltered inlets away from rough seas that slid into shore and far from deeper water frequented by men in single timber-hewn dugout canoes, or *mishoonash*. The men fished for eels, which they considered "juicy and sweet."[29] They fished in both salt and fresh water.

On Capawack, later named Martha's Vineyard, lived the Wampanoag, and their homes—wigwams—were made of woven marsh reeds over a cedar sapling frame, shaped like beehives. Wind and rain failed to intrude into interior floors, and smoke left from the place where wooden poles were bound together to support the structure; these homes were ingenious for providing cooling in summer and warmth in winter.[30]

Stone tools had a degree of sophistication and function, and on Capawack they were fashioned into spear points, arrowheads and hammers fastened with strips of rawhide to hardwood. Fishhooks were artfully made of bone and gently lowered into the inlets and coves of Nantucket Sound.[31] Crafting fishing nets blended art and science: plant fibers and certain inner barks were spun into cordage for weaving.[32]

Clothing was artfully sewn of deerskin, and furred animal skins became blankets. But unlike for mainland natives, there were fewer animals on Capawack, so woven native reeds, skins and furs were not used at all for house coverings. In winter, people moved to inland areas for shelter from strong ocean winds. Life revolved around tradition and the seasons. The Wampanoag belonged to the Algonquian linguistic family, which ranged from the Carolinas to Labrador and to the west nearly to the Great Lakes.[33]

To the east, five thousand years ago, before the sea level rose, Nantucket was a mere series of hills until ocean currents gave the island its distinctive shape. Wampanoag on Nantucket tended fish weirs in inlets, but later, by the late Woodland period, between one thousand and four hundred years ago, farming and hunting were added to fishing, as well as gathering. Their lives were remarkably similar to those of their relatives on Capawack.[34]

The Wampanoag population on Capawack and Nantucket believed that their existence was owed to Moshop, also spelled Moshup, the peace-loving, kindly "Great Chief," a giant who created land and provided food. And these were a people at peace with, and in harmony in, what nature provided.[35] The Wampanoag people's identity, the way their lives played out, was tied to Nantucket Sound. The tribes of the Wampanoag nation on Capawack were cultures embedded in tradition, myth and custom. And they never tired of sharing stories about Mich-a-bo, the Great White Hare, the founder of their medicine hut who was responsible for their creation and lived in the heavens.[36] All Wampanoag worshipped about thirty-seven gods, from Squauanit, the Woman's God, to Nanepaushat, the Moon's God.[37]

Before the white settlers arrived and permanently colonized Martha's Vineyard, the island was divided into four native administrative districts distinguished by natural boundaries and terrain and led by sachems, or chiefs.[38] These leaders weren't necessarily themselves born on the Vineyard, but their titles were hereditary and transferable, and it's likely that an off-island high-ranking Algonquin sachem chose them to rule over Chappaquiddick, Nunnepaug, Takemmy and Aquiniuh, which today is Gay Head.[39] The four—Pahkepunnassoo, Tweanticut, Mankutoukquet and Nohtooksaet, respectively—then subdivided their quadrants into "petty sachemships," and communal order was efficiently and strictly kept. This was a sophisticated method of governance.[40]

Wampanoag tribes on Capawack include the Chaubaqueduck on nearby Chappaquiddick. The Nashamoiess were established in the southern part of the island, and the Nashanekammuck lived at Chilmark. Near Edgartown were the Sanchecantacket, and the Ohkonkemme were near Tisbury. Their numbers dwindled after "the settlers brought diseases and many Indians died. Their burial places are scattered and often are marked only by field stones not always recognized as grave sites," wrote Dorothy R. Scoville in *Indian Legends of Martha's Vineyard*.[41]

Recorded history often tangos with informed legend or what we think, even hope, happened. The exploration canon of confirmed data is vivid but not expansive. We have the accounts of Gosnold, John Smith of Pocahontas fame and Samuel de Champlain, among the better known. However, while we may never confirm fact from fancy, these legends are worth mentioning and exploring. What of the oft lore: were Vikings in Nantucket Sound? Norse legend and sagas may provide seemingly vivid and familiar land and sea descriptions, but making the leap from what we think and what we can prove may forever be out of our grasp without conclusive proof.

Viking expedition literature describes and details foreign voyages, and there's little doubt or argument that Scandinavians explored this continent's coast. But whether the Norse explored Nantucket Sound or Bass River, which is part of Viking lore, has not been proven.

The culture on Capawack seemed timeless, driven by season, clan and community, until European monarchs grew restless and funded explorations to the North American coastline, seeking fresh frontiers and their riches, new lands to further domains. This, after all, was the nature of dominance. Competition among would-be discoverers was as fierce as fire; in their time, explorers were elevated to "rock star" status. In all probability, the Italian navigator Giovanni da Verrazzano sailed past Martha's Vineyard and Nantucket, and may have landed on either island, during his known voyage to New York Harbor and in and around Narragansett Bay.[42]

It is widely believed that Block Island, Rhode Island, in Narragansett Bay was his destination. Verrazzano wrote: "We found about twenty small boats of the people which, with divers cries and wonderings, came about our ship; coming no nearer than fifty paces towards us, they stared and beheld the artificialness of our ship, our shape and apparel, then they all made a loud shout together, declaring that they rejoiced."[43]

After Verrazzano, the continuum of culture on Capawack was forever altered in 1602 when the canvas sails of the bark *Concord*, captained by Bartholomew Gosnold, appeared off the horizon of Capawack, or the "refuge place." Nothing about the lives of the three thousand Native Americans on Capawack would be the same. On that voyage, Gosnold named Cape Cod for the abundance of codfish in the Sound. He apparently did not think, according to Wampanoag expert Linda Coombs, to ask the Wampanoag if the Sound had a native name.[44] Joining Gosnold's company for the voyage were two journalists, and one, John Brereton, we can thank for chronicling the journey.

Gosnold also named Capawack "Marthaes Vineyard," in honor of his eldest child, Martha, who was christened at Bury St. Edmunds in Suffolk, England, on April 24, 1597. Gosnold himself died on a later voyage to Virginia and was buried at Jamestown in 1607.

Samuel de Champlain sailed near Marthaes Vineyard on a ship bearing a French flag in 1606. While passing Cape Cod, de Champlain named the then peninsula Cape Malebarre, meaning the harbor inside of Monomoy near Nantucket Sound.[45] Venturing west through the Sound, de Champlain sailed past Capawack. Captain Adrian Block—of Block Island fame— was reputed to have stepped onto the Vineyard in 1614.[46] That same year, Captain John Smith ventured into Cape Cod waters, presumably at Nauset, to the east of the official boundaries of Nantucket Sound, in 1614.

John Smith, who had established an outpost in Virginia in 1607, sailed Cape Cod waters in 1614. On his way back to England, he left one of his men, Thomas Hunt, in charge of harvesting sassafras. During exploration, Hunt kidnapped about twenty-four native men whom he had lured onboard his ship. Captain Smith later wrote:

> *But one Thomas Hunt, the Master of this ship (when I was gone), thinking to prevent the intent I had to make there a Plantation, thereby to keepe this abounding Countrey still in obscuritie, that onely he and some few Merchants might enjoy wholly the Trade and profit of this Countrey, betrayed foure and twenty of those poore Salvages aboord his ship; and most dishonestly and inhumanely, for their kinde usage of me and all our men, carried them with him to Maligo, and there for a little private gaine sole those silly Salvages for Rialls of eight; but this vilde act kept him ever after from any more employment in those parts.*

A Vineyard native, Epenow, was among those abducted. But he would return to his native land with a vengeance against the English. Captain Edward Harlow is thought to have been the second white European to visit Capawack. He had taken Coneconam and Epenow of Capawack to be put into slavery, and along with three other natives, the company sailed for England through Nantucket Sound. In London, Harlow exhibited Epenow, known as a good and brave man, "stout, and sober in his demeanor." Shrewd, Epenow convinced his captors that gold on Martha's Vineyard was theirs if he would be returned to show them this treasure. Once back on his home shores, Epenow planned to escape. Harlow agreed to the gold expedition. The Earl of Southampton financed a third voyage to Capawack, and during the planning stages, Epenow was lodged at the London home of Sir

Ferdinando Gorges. A Maine Indian called Assacomet, a servant of Gorges, oversaw Epenow, and the two communicated despite varying dialects.

In June 1614, the ship sailed for Capawack with Harlow aboard. A Captain Hobson, who partially financed the voyage, sailed with Assacomet, Epenow and a third Indian whose name was either Manawet or Wenape. Once the vessel reached the American coast and before the travelers reached Capawack, through visits with other native pilots, Epenow, Assacomet and Manawet learned that another explorer, Thomas Hunt, had kidnapped natives at Patuxet, Plymouth and the Cape just several weeks prior. Adding to the increasingly negative dynamic, Manawet died under mysterious circumstances.

Hobson's vessel neared Capawack. Eager to trade with the English, native men boarded, including Epenow's brothers and cousins. After discussions with Epenow, his kin promised to return on a trading mission the next day. Twenty canoes appeared the following morning with close to one hundred native men in them, all armed with steady bows, but no attempt was made to fight. According to Gorges:

> *The captain speaks to Epenow to come to him where he was, in the forecastle of the ship. He then being in the waist of the ship, between two of the gentlemen that had him in guard, starts suddenly from them and coming to the captain, calls to his friends in English to come aboard; in the interim slips himself overboard, and although he was taken hold of one of the company, yet being a strong, heavy man, could not be stayed, and was no sooner in the water but the natives sent such a shower of arrows, and withal came so desperately near the ship, that they carried him away in spite of all the musketeers aboard, who were for the number as good as our nation did afford.*[47]

Despite his escape, Epenow's plan caused the slaughter of many Wampanoag and injuries to several aboard the ship. Hobson turned his vessel around, and he and Harlow made way for England with no gold.

The first white man believed to have interacted with the Wampanoag was Captain Thomas Dermer, who in 1616 visited the esteemed sachem Massasoit.[48] Dermer's visit took place a year after the 1617 epidemic, possibly smallpox, which decimated the Wampanoag population.

About 1642, the Reverend Thomas Mayhew persuaded the Wampanoag to trade native religion for Christianity. The first Wampanoag on Martha's Vineyard to be genuinely converted was Hiacoomes, who lived near Great Harbor (later Vineyard Haven). Thomas Mayhew Jr., then only twenty-four years old, became close friends with Hiacoomes and his family. It was from Hiacoomes that Mayhew learned the native language.

In 1657, Mayhew, then thirty-four, planned a trip home to England to report on his work with the Wampanoag, and to purchase additional supplies and books and bring more ministers to Martha's Vineyard.[49] Not far from Nantucket Sound, Mayhew held a last meeting with the Indians he had converted to Christianity. He opened the service with a prayer from the twenty-third psalm: "The Lord is my shepherd; I shall not want…" Peter Folger, the grandfather of Benjamin Franklin and whose great-great-grandson would be one of the first scientists to study Cape Cod waters, was charged with the Wampanoag ministry in Mayhew's absence.

Tragically, Mayhew's ship was presumed lost with all hands, including Thomas Mayhew's brother-in-law and the first native graduate of Harvard College, Joel Iacoomes, the son of the first Wampanoag on the Vineyard who embraced Christianity.[50]

Mayhew's father, the governor and founder of the island community, was a spry sixty-five-year-old who had reluctantly reclaimed the leadership mantle from his lost son. The governor's grandson, the Reverend John Mayhew, and John's son, Experience, another minister, carried on the family business devoted to the Vineyard's praying Wampanoag. A famed "constant preacher," the Reverend Experience Mayhew wrote of the natives' virtues in a volume of remembrances in 1830. Mayhew's benefactors lauded the minister's work and believed that a religious Native American benefitted white society: "Most certainly, to humanize the miserable, which our first English planters found surviving the wasting plagues which had so swept away the Indians, as to make room for a better people, to tame and civilize them, was a task of no little difficulty."[51] It is clear that Mayhew failed to regard the Wampanoag as equal human beings with an inherent right to their own ways and beliefs.[52]

Assannooshque was born into a culture hewn by her forbearers. But she died in 1708, an old woman acclimated to a life alongside the English, who had renamed her Old Sarah. She was known to have kept her wigwam "in very good repair." She was the widow of a native the English called James Cowkeeper. In her widowhood, Old Sarah provided well for her children. Reverend Experience Mayhew noted that she would visit the ill, feed the hungry and "took particular care of poor fatherless and motherless children." When she died, both English and Wampanoag mourned Assannooshque.

A Native American, Mechim, called his daughter Wuttontaetunnoo, whom the white settlers on Capawack renamed Katherine. Following her conversion to Christianity in her younger years, "she would, on the sight of a minister coming to preach in the place where she lived, discover all the signs of joy and reverence, proper to be manifested towards a person coming in the name of the Lord to a people." Katherine, formerly Wuttontaetunnoo, lived to old age but was "deranged" in her final year of life, dying in 1718 in Edgartown.

Visitors to Nantucket Sound's Islands in the seventeenth century provided detailed descriptions of the Wampanoag:

> *They are tall of body, proper and straight, of complexion swarthy and tawny…they all have black haire, brought to a more jetty color by oyling, dying and daily dressing…cut of divers forms according to their people. Sometimes they weare it very long…otherwise tied up hard and short like a horse's tail, bound up in a filet which they say makes it grow the faster: they are not a little fantastical or customsick in this particular. Other cuts they have as their fancy befools them, which would torture the wits of a curious Barber to imitate.*[53]

Like their brethren on Capawack, Native Americans on Nantucket belonged to the Wampanoag Nation. Thirty villages adhered to the rules of the top tier of management, the sachems. As in European monarchies, successors to the throne were hereditary. When no son was living, reins of leadership passed to daughters.

Wampanoag men plied the waters of Nantucket Sound in dugout canoes and were known as skilled boatmen: "All made in one piece, very easy to upset…Their cannows be made either of Pine-trees, which they burned hollow, scraping them smooth with Clam-shels and Oyster-shels, cutting their out-sides with stone hatchets. These Boats be not above a foot and a halfe, or two feet wide, and twenty foote long."[54]

Thirty men could fit into one canoe, and "instead of oares, they use Paddles and sticks with which they row faster than our Barges."[55]

Like the English, Nanahumake (later renamed Nantucket) Native Americans evolved into tradesmen, entering white capitalist fields such as formal carpentry and offshore whaling, though not as captains, since the English believed that working for a Wampanoag was beneath them. When natives died, their households were inventoried, as were the homes of the English settlers, in accordance with Nantucket law. Through records of yesteryear of newly deceased Wampanoag, the recorded contents of homes shed light as to their professions. In 1740, Mattakachame Micah died and the inventory showed him to be a carpenter: "With a broad axe, hatchet, carpenter's adz, hand saw, iron square, drawing knife, spike gimlets, a

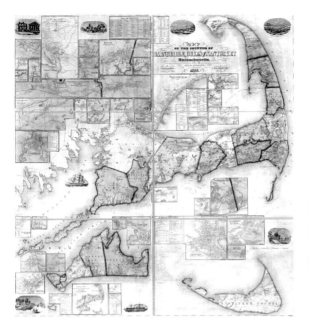

Henry F. Walling's famous 1858 map of Barnstable, Dukes and Nantucket Counties was cutting-edge for its day and vividly detailed businesses, schools, homes and churches. *Courtesy of the William Brewster Nickerson Room, Cape Cod Community College.*

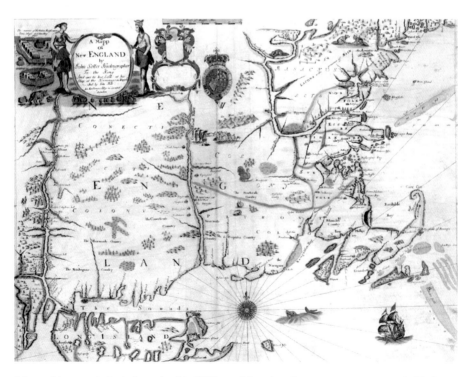

Mapmaking was in its infancy in this 1675 rendition, but the accuracy was remarkable for its time. *Courtesy of the Norman B. Leventhal Map Center, Boston Public Library.*

ladder, trowel, 2 chisels and 10 casks."[56] According to Linda Coombs of the Wampanoag Indigenous Programs at Plimoth Plantation, "This makes it sound like Micah made a choice to live like the English, versus the pressure of colonization."

On Nantucket, the remaining Wampanoag huddled in the Miacomet region were threatened with collapse during the winter of 1763–64. Of the remaining Indians on Nantucket who died during the sickness, 75 percent were adults, according to Nathaniel Philbrick in *Abram's Eyes, the Native American Legacy of Nantucket Island.*[57] "It began with a severe headache, soon followed by a yellowing of the skin and eyes, the yellow turning to a livid white just prior to death as the sufferer lapsed into a feverish delirium," recounted Philbrick.[58] It appeared that only the Indians were affected, and the white population of Nantucket was untouched.[59] Thirty-four Indians who did fall ill eventually recovered.[60] Natives untouched were the ones at sea or those living in less populated native sections of Nantucket. Whatever the disease was, it reduced Nantucket's native population to a low from which the population could not reclaim kin or clan, or recover its numbers.

In 1797, more than a century after the English had come to permanently settle on Nantucket, the last wigwam on old Nanahumake was dismantled on Tristram Starbuck's farm, a dwelling Abigail Fisher lived in.[61] The last native on Nantucket was Abram Quary, who passed on in the town's poorhouse on November 25, 1854, at the age of eighty-two.[62]

Today, the existing Capawack Wampanoag live in the bustling native community of Aquinnah on Martha's Vineyard.

.

# Chapter Three

# COLONIES AND CAPITALISM

*People don't understand what colonization means, and the impact it has on those*
*colonized. It's a process that forcefully changes our whole way of life.*
—Linda Coombs, *Wampanoag Indigenous Programs, Plimoth Plantation*

*I wish I could be acquainted with the feelings and thoughts which must agitate the heart*
*and present themselves to the mind of an enlightened Englishman, when he first lands*
*on this continent. He must greatly rejoice that he lived at a time to see this fair country*
*discovered and settled; he must necessarily feel a share of national pride, when he views*
*the chain of settlements which embellishes these extended shores. When he says to himself,*
*this is the work of my countrymen, who, when convulsed by factions, afflicted by a*
*variety of miseries and wants, restless and impatient, took refuge here. They brought*
*along with them their national genius, to which they principally owe what liberty they*
*enjoy, and what substance they possess. Here he sees the industry of his native country*
*displayed in a new manner, and traces in their works the embrios of all the arts, sciences,*
*and ingenuity which flourish in Europe. Here he beholds fair cities, substantial villages,*
*extensive fields, an immense country filled with decent houses, good roads, orchards,*
*meadows, and bridges, where a hundred years ago all was wild, woody and uncultivated!*
*What a train of pleasing ideas this fair spectacle must suggest; it is a prospect which*
*must inspire a good citizen with the most heartfelt pleasure.*
—Letters from an American Farmer, *J. Hector St. John Crevecoeur*

S lowly the small boats and larger ships came and then dozens and
hundreds more, bringing with them Europeans eager to claim, control
and conquer lands along Nantucket Sound from Cape Cod to Martha's
Vineyard and Nantucket. They sailed on the heels of explorers who had
merely passed through, including Verrazzano, Adrian Block, John Smith
and Samuel de Champlain.

In 1659, the Puritan Thomas Mayhew bartered with the Wampanoag on Nanahumake and sold rights to their former lands to a group of nine settlers, all English, some Quakers, from New Hampshire and Massachusetts.[63] Their goal was to establish an independent community outside of the privity of Puritan oversight. Mayhew kept the business deal in the family: Mayhew's cousin, Thomas Macy, and Tristram Coffin, the founder of that famous island clan, were among the first to come to Nantucket.[64] Macy and his company of landholders shared the island with an estimated three thousand Native Americans who were established in their own trades of farming, hunting, fishing and shore whaling.[65]

The first housing lottery to the original twenty families of settlers was held in 1661.[66] It's believed that the earliest settlement date was in July 1661, about midsummer. Within ten years, other white settlers arrived with familiar surnames such as Coleman, Barnard, Bunker, Hussey, Starbuck, Swain, Worth and Folger.[67]

The social science of civic planning was rudimentary at best, though certainly Macy and others in senior leadership positions within the community relied on the lottery system for nonbiased distribution of lands. Historian William Root Bliss distinguished between former lands and this new sea-bound property for Nanahumake's first white residents: "They looked upon their island estate as a vast farm securely fenced from wild beasts by the ocean. Its forests of oak, walnut, beech, pine, and cedar trees were ready to give timber for their houses…the neck contained fresh meadows; through which a brook was running; patches of white-oak trees; and a great swamp skirted by cranberry vines."[68]

These former farmers retrained for new careers. Thomas Macy entered the weaving trade; William Worth, Joseph Coleman and Richard Gardner became seamen; Nathaniel Holland was Nantucket's first tailor; and Joseph Gardner was suddenly responsible "as a Shoomaker." John Savidge was one of the few who retained his original trade as a cooper, or barrel maker.[69]

One year later, Nantucket was a true home to the core founding families and leaders who began to record vital statistics. In the first fifteen years, six individuals had died, seventy-four births were recorded and the nuptials of Mary Coffin and Nathaniel Starbuck were celebrated.[70]

Eventually, Nanahumake became Nantucket.[71] In June 1665, a public meeting was held, at which the sachem Attaphehat, with all the Tomokonoth natives, acknowledged the English government of Nantucket and did "owne them selves subjects to King Charles the Second." The Native American leader of Mount Hope, the sachem Metacomet, was present.

By 1668–69, Macy and other English struck a deal with Native Americans working the thriving drift whaling business on Nantucket Sound. Nantucket's shore was divided into sections for Native Americans and English, with the spoils to be shared. Cultures clashed and people did not get along. One dispute that ended in court was resolved when a jury of six men found for the plaintiff, a native named Massaquat, who accused Eleaser Foulger of stealing his drift whale. Foulger confessed that he "did dispose of the Whale in controversie," for which the court fined him "to pay for the Whale the summe of four pounds in goods at the usual price of trading."[72]

Whaling ships drew at least nine feet, potentially a danger for vessels leaving the fickle shoals of Nantucket Sound.[73] Eighty years would pass before Congress finally approved funds to construct a riprap jetty to outsmart the dangerous Nantucket Bar, the monstrous shoal that prevented heavily laden vessels from docking without the use of lighters.[74] By 1884, a western jetty extending four thousand feet into Nantucket Sound was complete; tons of granite boulders were brought from Maine. It would be another ten years before work was approved for an eastern jetty to flank Nantucket Harbor's entrance.[75]

Nantucket's vessels were considered American commercial ambassadors, famous the world over. Captain James Cary (1777–1812) used the Nantucket-built ship *Rose* to become the first island vessel dedicated to exclusive China trade.[76]

The French-American writer J. Hector St. John de Crevecoeur visited Nantucket and Martha's Vineyard while touring his adopted country. His breakthrough book of essays, *Letters from an American Farmer*, lifted Crevecoeur to celebrity status and was the first book by an American to be a success in Europe:

> *Would you believe that a sandy spot of about twenty-three thousand acres, affording neither stones nor timber, meadows nor arable, yet can boast of an handsome town consisting of more than 500 houses, should possess above 200 sail of vessels, constantly employ upwards of 2000 seamen; feed more than 15,000 sheep, 500 cows, 200 horses; and has several citizens worth 20,000L. sterling!*[77]

By 1650, English families with surnames such as Butler, Folger, Norton and Pease had settled on Martha's Vineyard and began homesteads by purchasing land from the Wampanoag.[78] Dukes County was incorporated on November 1, 1668.

Cape Cod towns lining Nantucket Sound were geographically distinct but shared common culture. Beginning as small satellite communities from the

Vineyard Haven was a hive of maritime activity on Nantucket Sound. *Courtesy of Detrick Lawrence Productions.*

Plymouth colony, core families intermarried for generations and eventually grew to form their own municipalities. Most of these were incorporated within a handful of years of one another. Larger towns split into additional communities following political growing pains. For instance, in 1793, Yarmouth's "east parish" separated into a new community, the town of Dennis, named for the long-serving Minister Josiah Dennis. In 1803, the "north parish" of Harwich petitioned the Massachusetts legislature for independence and incorporated as the town of Brewster. The only exception is the town of Mashpee, which was incorporated as a Native American town in 1870 alongside Gay Head on Martha's Vineyard.

In 1661, Isaac Robinson journeyed to an area the natives called Succonesset and built himself a small home on four acres of land between Fresh and Salt Ponds, and in doing so he became the first settler of the town of Falmouth; later in 1661, Jonathan Hatch would join Robinson.[79] The first comers to Succonesset laid out lot lines, some of which were "lying on the sea and running 200 rods towards the woods."[80] A rod is an English method popular during colonial times to measure land and is equal to 5.5 yards or 16.5 feet.[81]

By June 1668, the settlement was incorporated as a township, but the name "Falmouth" did not appear on official records until September 1694.[82]

Falmouth was unfortunately near British bases in nearby Vineyard Sound during the Revolutionary War. Undersupplied English marines continually raided livestock and food from weary Falmouth. But Falmouth had a strong militia led by Major Joseph Dimmick, who led four local companies and beat back an English advance on April 3, 1779, with no casualties on the American side except for one cannonball fired into a town building.

Katharine Lee Bates, the Wellesley college professor, poet and author of "America the Beautiful," spent most of her childhood years in Falmouth, where her father, William Bates, was minister of the First Congregational Church on the Village Green. Her teenage years and adulthood were spent off Cape, but Ms. Bates was buried at the Oak Grove Cemetery in Falmouth following her death in March 1929 at the age of sixty-nine.

Woods Hole's contributions to the Nantucket Sound community are in boat building and whaling. The Swift family in Falmouth, led by Elijah Swift and his son, Oliver Cromwell Swift, ruled local whaling:

> *In the period of the greatest whaling activity from Falmouth, from 1831 to 1848, the Swift interests outfitted twenty-four vessels, while other Falmouth vessels made fourteen voyages. Elijah and Oliver had at least a controlling interest in the* Sarah Herrick, *the* Pocahontas, *the* Uncas, *the* Awashonks, *the* Brunette, *the* Hobomok, *the* William Penn, *and the* Commodore Morris. *These vessels with an aggregate tonnage of 2,558 tons represented more than two thirds of the vessels to sail from Falmouth. While some of these vessels such as the* William Penn *were divided into 64ths for ownership, others such as the* Commodore Morris *were owned by a very few; in the case of the* Commodore Morris *by Elijah, his son-in-law, Henry Bunker, Oliver, and Oliver's brother-in-law, John Jenkins.*[83]

Elijah contracted with the U.S. Navy to provide live oak for naval construction.[84]

Given its strategically convenient location from south to north, Nantucket Sound played an unwitting role in ferrying escaped slaves to freedom in the North on the Underground Railroad, with certainty. In truth, the number of abolitionists on Cape Cod and the Islands far outnumbered supporters of slavery, outlawed in Massachusetts since 1783:

> *There was an Underground Railroad station in New Bedford where fugitive slaves, having arrived as stowaways on coastal vessels, were helped to*

The old customhouse in Woods Hole, Falmouth's village at the western edge of Nantucket Sound. *Courtesy of the Falmouth Historical Society.*

*Canada and freedom. Such incidents occurred very rarely on the Vineyard. But in September 1854 at Holmes Hole a black man, said to be a fugitive slave, escaped during the night from the vessel on which he had stowed away in Florida. The captain, when the stowaway revealed himself during the voyage, stopped at Holmes Hole to turn him over to the customs officer. Unfamiliar with the procedure, the Holmes Hole officer wrote to the Boston collector for advice. One night, before a response from Boston had been received, the slave escaped.*[85]

An industry unique to Falmouth from 1863 through 1889 was the Pacific Guano Works in the village of Woods Hole at Long Neck, now Penzance Point.[86] A Dennis native, Prince S. Crowell, struck upon the idea of using guano—accumulated fowl dung—and mixing it with menhaden, "from which the oil had been extracted, and add a small amount of other chemicals to make the best possible fertilizer" for commercial properties, according to the *Falmouth Enterprise.*

The Pacific Guano Works, for which many Irish immigrants worked, owned thirty-three vessels that hauled bird dung from the Howland Islands in the Pacific back to Woods Hole.[87] Crowell's company saw immense success, shipping 7,540 two-hundred-pound bags by 1865.[88] In business, supply and demand drives success, and when the Howland Islands supply ran low, Crowell closed up shop and fewer dung-laden vessels sailed into Nantucket Sound. Later, dung deposits in the Caribbean Sea off Honduras continued to supply the demand for this fertilizer.[89]

Norman T. Allen wrote that "the production of fertilizer reached approximately 40,000 tons annual in the late 1870's." Cotton and tobacco growers and gardeners, especially in Virginia, were regular customers of this concoction made of scrap fish parts, chemicals and foreign bird dung. For the foreign, native harvesters, this profession was extremely harmful to their health; the strong ammonia fumes slowly blinded them.

The smell meandering through Woods Hole during the Pacific Guano Works' years of operation was as bad as you can imagine. Hands down, ripe guano was the nastiest cargo in shipping. One person compared the stench to the infamous stockyards of Chicago when winds blew west.[90]

Woods Hole and Nantucket Sound are deeply connected. Scientific institutions that have put Woods Hole on the map, so to speak, are there, in part, because of proximity to Nantucket Sound.[91] In 1871, the new commissioner of fisheries for the federal government, Spencer F. Baird, chose Woods Hole for the agency's new headquarters at Great Harbor, which was completed in 1884. Baird's office, the U.S. Fish Commission, studied ways to manage fisheries and conserve harvestable stocks.

The Marine Biological Laboratory—MBL to locals—was incorporated in 1888 and is the second laboratory in Woods Hole.[92] Founding organizations and individuals of MBL were the Woman's Education Association of Boston, the Boston Society of Natural History and professors from Harvard University, the Massachusetts Institute of Technology and Williams College.[93]

Woods Hole's reputation as a summer resort equaled its scientific renown; Falmouth today has eleven public beaches. As the story goes, a Boston merchant, Joseph Story Fay, bought the first summer house in Woods Hole, the property of Ward Parker, overlooking Little Harbor.[94] More tourists arrived when the Old Colony Railroad was extended to Woods Hole. The McMansions of their day began going up in the 1870s and 1880s at Nobska and Juniper Points.[95] Long since torn down were two huge hotels, the Webster House and the Dexter House, which served summer tourist traffic.

In 1896, the name of Woods Hole became official, deriving from "Wood's Holl-holl," Scandinavian for "harbor." From 1789 to 1913, according to the Falmouth Historical Society, Woods Hole was part of the Barnstable Customs District.

One additional scientific facility came to Woods Hole in 1930: the famed Woods Hole Oceanographic Institution. Norman T. Allen wrote in 1966:

Fisheries science had its beginnings at the U.S. Fish Commission in Woods Hole. *Courtesy of the Falmouth Historical Society.*

*In the late 1920's the National Academy of Sciences appointed a Committee on Oceanography to study the role which the United States should play in a world-wide oceanographic research program. Conferences were held in the summer of 1928 at Woods Hole and persons representing several universities and existing marine laboratories attended. Dr. Henry B. Bigelow was asked to study and report on the problems and importance of ocean research. This report recommended the establishment of a fully equipped oceanographic*

*laboratory on the Atlantic Coast and it also recommended that the sum of $3,000,000 should be provided. The project was transferred to the Rockefeller which granted authority to their Executive Committee to aid in the support of the project. A group of thirteen persons was chosen to serve as Trustees and corporation members until the first annual meeting.*[96]

Just west of Falmouth is the Wampanoag town of Mashpee, whose boundary from the former Succonesset was not determined until April 1725.[97] More than five miles of sandy beach line Nantucket Sound, and wondrously large stretches of waterfront are on Popponesset and Waquoit Bays. Mashpee's history on Nantucket Sound is deeply interwoven with Native Americans.

On October 21, 1639, the Reverend John Lothrop, a beloved but stern cleric, and many family groups arrived on Cape Cod to settle the town of Barnstable, with southern borders reaching north from Cape Cod Bay to Nantucket Sound.[98] Actual incorporation occurred on September 3, 1639. The area was deeply wooded, with solid populations of bear and wolf. Peaceful Wampanoag were established nearby. Following the reverend into the wilderness were Messrs. Mayo, Lumbard Sr. and men whose first names are part of the official record: Isaac Wells, Samuel Hinckley, Samuel Fuller, Robert Shelley, Edward Fitzrandal, Henry Ewell, Henry Rowley, James Cudworth, William Crocker, John Cooper, Henry Cobb, George Lewis, Robert Linnell, William Parker, Edward Caseley, William Caseley, Henry Bourne, Anthony Annable, Austin Bearse and Isaac Robinson, along with their wives and children.[99] A handful of these surnames remain part of the Barnstable community today. No fewer than twenty-five other heads of families arrived, and before long, land was sliced into portions on the northern side of Barnstable; it wasn't until 1644 that the southwest portion of the community was settled.

Miles Standish brokered real estate deals with native sachems on behalf of English colonists who settled Cape Cod under permission from the Plymouth Colony. It is said that the Wampanoag had a nickname for the pugnacious Standish: "Captain Shrimp." At any rate, on behalf of Reverend Lothrop, Standish oversaw land purchases that would formally extend Barnstable's municipal lands to Nantucket Sound. The Wampanoag viewed land as a shared resource, never to be fenced in and open to all who needed to hunt, walk or pass through. They did not have in their language words to describe "bought." Slowly, the natives began to sell their ancestral lands.

"Serunk," a Wampanoag "South Sea chief" for whom little information was available, was reportedly paid "four coats and three axes" for acreage along Nantucket Sound on August 26, 1644.[100] Serunk made a mark on the deed, which was witnessed by Anthony Annable, Henry Cobb, Thomas Allen, John Smith, Laurence Willis and Thomas Dimock.[101] A second land purchase occurred in 1647 when Thomas Dimock and Isaac Robinson gave Nepoyetum two coats and a promise of plowing. It's unclear whether this land was on Barnstable's north or south side. In 1648, a South Sea Indian named Paupmunnuck sold Miles Standish "the southern part of the town from the Mashpee line east to the Oyster river, and to Iyanough or Ianno's lands on the east, and to Nepoyetum's lands on the north." The price?

Two brass kettles and promised fencing work. Barnstable drew its identity primarily from the sea despite the dense woodland in its boundaries.[102]

The Crosby family of Osterville established the venerable Crosby Boatyard in 1850. Brothers Charles, Horace and Worthington began tinkering with boat designs following the death of their father, Andrew, who was constructing coasting vessels when he died in 1837 at forty-two. Years later, their daring design, a "catboat" about eighteen feet long, ably navigated shoals with a unique centerboard design. Writer Stan Grayson said, "The best information available suggests that the first Crosby catboat appeared between 1857 and 1860 and was the end result of at least a decade of development influenced by centerboard-equipped, jib-and-mainsail boats in New York and centerboard boats in Rhode Island."[103]

Like Chatham today, the Barnstable village of Osterville shares a reputation for exclusive shops and high real estate prices, but the true roots of these communities lie in respective roles in maritime history and culture:

Worthington Crosby (center, white beard) of the famous Crosby Boatyard in Osterville poses with his crew. *Courtesy of Osterville Historical Society.*

Chatham for fishing, and Osterville for the Crosby Boatyard and its long, distinguished list of sea captains from many families. It is widely thought that Osterville is named for its old nickname of Oyster Island Village, which later became Oysterville or Osterville.[104] Reaching further back in time, the Indian sachem Paupmunnuck led a tribe called Cotachese on land that is now Osterville. Many native names to describe the area emanated from the Wampanoag word *chunkoo*, or oyster, as many of these shellfish were harvested from Osterville's mud flats.[105] A saltworks on the shores of Osterville's East Bay was in operation in 1812 with vats owned by Thomas Ames, Seth Goodspeed, George Hinckley, Henry Lovell, Jacob Lovell, Deacon Josiah Scudder Sr. and George Lovell, according to Paul Chesbro.[106]

Once settled, the truth is that this village, like others on Cape Cod, had its economic ups and downs yet hosted a healthy fishing community. A series of news items taken from the pages of the *Barnstable Patriot* in the nineteenth century, compiled by Paul Chesbro, is a testament to Osterville's simpler times. These news stories provide snapshots of a productive community along the shores of Nantucket Sound:

November 20, 1877: "Our pogie fishermen have nearly all arrived home."
August 26, 1879:

> *The storm landed many boats high on marshes, but most of them have been launched again in good order. The tide was the highest ever known. At Mrs. Seth Goodspeed's the water was about one foot deep in the barn and pig-sty, so the pig had to take refuge on the platform in the rear part of his quarters. Bath houses, wharf, etc., were washed away and some destroyed. The bank along with the shore was badly washed away, and between the Neck, so called, where we want a cut through, the sea washed over all along. H.N. Lovell had quite a dowery left him near his house. Nearly one-quarter of a mile from shore were tons of seaweed and drift stuff, boats, etc...At Capt. J.P. Hodges' two large trees were blown down, and at other places corn was destroyed.*

June 1, 1880: "Our little village is crowded with summer visitors."

Herbert W. Adams (1867–1893) was the only son and child of an Osterville couple, Watson F. and Susan Adams.[107] He was a beautiful boy with blue eyes and dark hair severely parted and combed over his left eye. In August 1887, when Herbert was twenty, he sailed with his maternal grandfather, Captain Nathan E. West Sr., a coasting skipper. The pair left Boston, spent a night anchored off Osterville on August 19 and left the next day for New York to pick up a cargo of coal, then recrossed Nantucket Sound back toward Boston.[108] Young Adams kept a journal of his trip, with excerpts following, revealing a firsthand account of life aboard a coastal schooner on Nantucket Sound. The journal begins on August 17, 1887, as Herbert and his grandfather, along with the crew, prepare to leave Boston Harbor:

August 17, 1887: "Our cook swore at the tug boat captain when he parted our hawser. The mate reprimanded him, and he got mad and he threatened to knock him down, but the captain interfered and quieted things down. But the cook says he is going to leave."

August 19, 1887: "Off Nauset. At 6 A.M., trying hard to get over the shoals with a head wind and head tide. At 12 Noon we anchored in Parker's harbor (Osterville). Went ashore. Went to C.F. Parker's and telephoned my mother. Went to the library fair and heard the band play."

August 21: "Rise at 5:15 A.M. Grandpa thinks we had better start at about 6 A.M. Got on vessel at 7 A.M. Left Parker's Harbor at 8 A.M. for New York. At 2 P.M. we are off Falmouth and it is raining hard."

August 22: "Captain said it was so dark in the night that the men would pass and not know it. At 9:30 P.M. we passed the Schooner *Lottie K.* Grandfather steered all night. He is too old to do that."

In early May 1893, Herbert fell ill. Over three weeks his health steadily declined, and he passed away on Saturday, May 30, at his parents' home in Osterville. Herbert was twenty-six years old.

A nineteenth-century view of the West Bay coastline, Osterville. *Courtesy of Osterville Historical Society.*

The Wampanoag lived on lands in present-day Yarmouth, but they called their home by different names: Mattacheese, Mattacheeset, Hockanom and Nobscusset.[109] In early 1639, the Plymouth Court granted Anthony Thacher, John Crow and Thomas Howes the authority to settle the land in a community later named Yarmouth, supposedly so named since the newcomers were from that seaside area of eastern England.[110] The following March, others joined the colony, including Hugh Tilley, Giles Hopkins and Joshua Barnes; William Clark was sworn in as constable.[111]

Tensions with Native Americans were an issue for Yarmouth residents, but it was not the Wampanoag who caused the ruckus; rather, it was the off-Cape Narragansett Native Americans with whom the colony court sent soldiers to fight in 1642 and 1645. While fifty-two Yarmouth men bore arms, only two "soldiers" were furnished to this regional effort.[112]

By 1778, the last of Yarmouth's Wampanoag had settled in a small section of South Yarmouth. Soon they would be pushed out from there. Selectmen that year ordered that their lands be sold "or hired out" to reimburse the town's coffers for the cost of bills associated with the smallpox epidemic, which had already decimated the small native population.

In Yarmouth, the first saltworks sprang up on Bass River on land that John Kelley sold to Isaiah Crowell, Seth Kelley and Zeno Kelley. Indeed, Bass River boasted acres of saltworks. John Sears of Dennis had invented the process by which salt was rendered from seawater, and in the early years his neighbors called the concept "Sears's Folly." How wrong they were, for in later years Sears would be lauded for his invention.

Coastal captains running packet vessels used Bass River to access West Dennis to offload coal, lumber, grain, flour and heavier merchandise. Hiram Loring was a businessman from Dennis who kept a regular packet vessel running to and from New York through Nantucket Sound.

By 1795, three wharves had been built on the east side of Bass River, the western boundary of Dennis. For the next seventy-five years, fishing for cod and mackerel was the chief occupation, except during wartime. Levi Eldridge's enterprise in West Chatham near the Harwich line cured and packed fish but abandoned the site in 1887. Chatham's boat works included the construction in 1835 of the schooners *Jew and Gentile* and *Emulous*.

Job Chase Jr. of West Harwich and his business partners, Richard Baker, Elijah Chase and Isaiah Chase, obtained permission from the Massachusetts legislature to build a pier six hundred feet into the Sound at the end of Depot Street in Dennis Port, beginning in 1834. At the end of the project, it was clear that "boats couldn't come in" to the pier at low tide, recounted historian Phyllis Horton, who is descended from the Dennis Port Robbins clan. So Chase and his cohorts offloaded onto smaller vessels to ferry goods and people to shore. By 1848, Chase won legislative approval for a new wharf six hundred feet in length, out to the pier, which solved the problem.[113] J.K. Baker's wharf was located at the end of present-day Sea Street, south of Dennis Port. Just east of Baker's Wharf was Anthony Kelley's Union Wharf.[114]

The 1850 census reveals that 715 Dennis men were employed on some or all of these three central wharves, and fifty-four vessels sailed in and out from their planks. Dennis was also a stopover for many vessels using Nantucket Sound. Dennis fishermen usually opted for mackerel, and these fishing vessels would continue on through the Sound to offload in New Bedford, Fall River, Providence and even as far south as Philadelphia and New York.

Farther west along the Dennis shore was Swan River, which divided West Dennis from Dennis Port, a site where Nathan Fisk constructed the bridge later rebuilt as the Lower County Bridge.

It should be noted that Dennis Port did not actually become Dennis Port until its official incorporation in 1863. Before 1863, the area was known simply as "Crocker's Neck." Local folks like general store owner Thomas

This windmill in Dennis Port stood for generations. *Courtesy of Burton N. Derick.*

Howes didn't fancy having to travel to neighboring West Harwich to pick up mail. Howes cooked up the idea to bring back the mail of people who did not shop in his store; they'd have to come in to pick up the post. His business grew, and in fact Howes was the person who named Dennis Port. Naturally, the first post office was located in his home.[115]

Dennis was one of those Cape Cod towns where villages were distinctly and fiercely independent. Rarely did residents of Bass River, the hamlet in South Yarmouth, walk or hitch the wagon for a trip to Yarmouth Port to the north, along Cape Cod Bay. "South side people fished out of south side ports, and north side people went to Boston, Salem and Portsmouth," Horton explained.[116] "Dennis mariners have always been able to make a living on the water whenever the opportunity presented itself—and Prohibition, for example, proved another opportunity. Hundreds or thousands of bottles and cans landed in Dennis to be distributed elsewhere, but a certain percentage found its way into Dennis cellars, barns and closets."

With Prohibition, there was no inhibition for Cape Codders to use the Sound to make extra cash. The Sound is filled with memories and reads like the pages of an American history textbook. On May 30, 1930, the Barnstable village of Osterville rumbled by the exchange of offshore firearms and the boom of a "heavy gun." Later it was learned that the ruckus was from a government boat chasing a rumrunner.[117] The outcome of the chase was never revealed.

The town of Dennis is a chief reason why Cape Cod has earned a reputation as quirky and independent, charmingly Yankee through and through. For generations, locals called certain areas of land abutting Nantucket Sound by names that do not appear on any map. For instance, "Battletown" is an area in South Village in West Dennis, near the mouth of Swan Pond River, that historian Burt Derick claims was a "rough neighborhood." And Bakertown, which is an extensive area on the south side of Dennis near the Sound, was so named for one of the first settlers, Francis Baker, who arrived about 1641, says Derick. At that time Dennis didn't exist, so the area was considered the eastern parish of Yarmouth. Dennis was not incorporated as a town until the early 1790s. Francis had six sons, many of whom established homesteads on land extending from Follins Pond south to Nantucket Sound, and slightly east and west.

Almost immediately after incorporation, expansion to the south side near Nantucket Sound began, particularly in Dennis Port, a noted fishing community.

*The oldest of the wharves, the westerly one, was built in 1849 by the grandfather and father of Samuel S. Baker, the present owner. The other wharf was built in 1888 and belongs to the Dennis Port Fishing Company, of which J.P. Edwards is the representative. The company started in 1885 with four new schooners, built at Essex, and from this wharf and the fitting store kept by Mr. Edwards, three of the vessels make trips in mackerel fishing and to the Banks for cod. In 1879 Nehemiah Wixon built and opened a grocery store on the street leading to the sound.*[118]

The nineteenth century could be called progressive in terms of fisheries management. It was noted that in 1888 the shad had returned to Nantucket Sound in healthy numbers "for the first time in many years," as one local noted. One thousand barrels of shad were harvested in the summer of 1888.[119]

Present-day Harwich used to include Brewster and Orleans, some of Eastham and probably a bit of Chatham before the colony court at Plymouth approved a grant on March 5, 1644–45. The exact wording is:

*The Court doth grant unto the church of New Plymouth, or those that go to dwell at Nauset all the tract of land lying between the sea and sea, from the purchasers' bounds at Namskaket to the Herring Brook at Billingsgate, with said Herring brook, and all the meadow on both sides of the said brook, with the great Bass pond there, and all the meadows and islands lying within said track.*[120]

Thomas Prence, John Doane, Nicholas Snow, Josiah Cook, Richard Higgins, John Smalley and Edward Bangs were the first settlers at Harwich, which was incorporated in 1694, and soon were joined by other Englishmen eager for a fresh start on Cape Cod.[121] They intended to farm and purchased land from the Indians in exchange for "moose skins, Indian coats, wampum, little knives, &c."[122]

Over the years, the "Harwiches" were settled by core families headed by men such as John Dillingham, Thomas Crosby and Thomas Snow, the latter two chosen as the first "fence-viewers" in town. A Congregational church, the so-called South Precinct Church, was located in Harwich proper, on the highest hill in town.[123] Common, or public, schools were eventually begun, and the Cape Cod Bank was founded, too.[124] A large hall for public lectures, a printing office for the new weekly, the *Cape Cod Republican*, and, according to historian Frederick Freeman, "other indispensible accompaniments of a well-ordered neighborhood, many neat residences," were established in Harwich. Other villages were North Harwich, West Harwich, South Harwich and Harwich Port, all near Nantucket Sound, and East Harwich, a bit north.[125]

Within years, many of the farmers who immigrated to Harwich began fishing, with elite mariners serving as captains of tall ships. By 1803, the "north parish" split from Harwich and was incorporated as the town of Brewster, which abuts Cape Cod Bay but has no southern Cape boundary. A key reason for the split, which still smarts in some reaches of Harwich today, was due to maritime class warfare of sorts. Up in the north parish, the majority of heads of households were merchant sea captains and their families, while day fishermen clustered in villages on Nantucket Sound.

By 1837, twenty vessels were registered in Harwich and fishermen caught ten thousand pounds of codfish, worth an estimated $30,000, and five hundred barrels of mackerel with a market price of $3,000.[126] Nine thousand bushels of salt were used to process the catch.[127] As Harwich matured, its prominent sea captains were active in civic circles, and the same was true in Nantucket Sound communities on Cape Cod, Martha's Vineyard and Nantucket.

Founders in every community on Nantucket Sound bartered with Wampanoag for land to turn ancient forest into farmland or preserve open meadows and pastures for grazing and sheep husbandry. It was no different in 1665, when William Nickerson "bought of John Quason, alias Towsomet,

Herring River, Harwich, circa 1944. *Courtesy of Burton N. Derick.*

West Chatham was on the extreme eastern edge of Nantucket Sound and was a noted fishing port. *Courtesy of Burton N. Derick.*

sachem of Monomoyick, a tract of land near Potanumaquut, bounded E. by the Great Harbor S., by a line which extends W. by S. into the woods from Weequasset to a pine-tree marked on four sides, and N. by a line extending to the further head of a ponds to a place called Porchommock."[128] An English name was attached to the area that we today call Chatham. In 1672, Nickerson expanded his range in exchange for "one shallop, ten coats of trucking-cloth, six kettles, twelve axes, twelve hoes, twelve knives, forty shillings in wampum, a hat, and twelve shillings in money."[129]

Only the extreme western edge of Chatham inside of Stage Harbor lies within Nantucket Sound, as well as the eastern slice of Monomoy. Stage Harbor is about a mile long and a half mile wide and is the entrance between Morris Island and Harding's Neck or Beach.

Chinese laborers harvested eelgrass off Monomoy and Harding's Beach in the late nineteenth century for use in the production of construction insulation—according to historian Richard Ryder—for Chelsea, Massachusetts businessman Samuel Cabot.

From its settlement on, the men of Chatham were farmers, growing rye, corn and English hay as staples. By 1711, fishing was a new occupation for the Chatham men, brought by Daniel Greenleaf, who removed from Yarmouth, began to fish at Monomoy and cured and packed what he caught.[130]

Wet fishing line is stored on a dock in Chatham's Stage Harbor. *Courtesy of Burton N. Derick.*

Thomas Sparrow, Joseph Reed and Isaiah Lewis formed a cooperative called Sparrow, Reed & Lewis in 1847, when they began to fish off Monomoy.[131] Others joined the fishing fleet, with Chatham having at least twenty-two fishing vessels. By 1855, Chatham's population was 2,560 and "was a relatively wealthy township," according to historian Frederick Freeman. When fisheries declined in the latter half of the nineteenth century, the humble red cranberry picked up the commercial slack in Chatham. Historian Burt Derick says that the "village" on the tip of Monomoy was called "White Wash City'" and proved ideal for "clamming and fishing trades."

Working the maritime trades on Nantucket Sound did not always require time at sea or trips away from home. Saltworks, shipbuilding, fish flakes— where fish were dried in the sun and then cured with salt—and smaller maritime industries such as net mending dotted the shore of inlets, coves, rivers and estuaries along the Sound. Rendering salt from evaporated seawater stored in giant wooden vats was a huge industry in almost every Nantucket Sound community. In Chatham, along the Sound, the saltworks in Stage Harbor belonged to William Hamilton, Christopher Taylor and Joseph and Isaiah Harding.[132]

Tourism evolved in the late nineteenth century in every community on Nantucket Sound on Cape Cod, Martha's Vineyard and Nantucket. The advent of steam fostered the notion that visitors to Nantucket Sound could relax while the locals labored in maritime industries.

In Nantucket Sound, the communities of Hyannis, Falmouth, Holmes Hole—now Vineyard Haven—Old Town on Martha's Vineyard and Shelburne on Nantucket felt the brunt of British wrath during the Revolutionary War. On May 11, 1775, John Linzee, commander of His Majesty's sloop *Falcon*, anchored at East Chop outside Holmes Hole and detained a Maryland trading ship "laden with flower and Corn." Nantucket had a desperate need for provisions "from the main." On October 9, 1776, smuggled into the harbor were "60 to 70 weight of Butter as much chees, 1 Cow dead, 2 Bbls Cyder, 3 Bushels Quinces—several Bushels Apples… Cheries, Peas, Apples &c, one deer, skin & all."[133]

For the men of Yarmouth, between Barnstable to the west and Dennis to the east, the call to arms came on or about June 20, 1776, when townsfolk "voted, that the inhabitants of Yarmouth do declare a state of independence of the King of Great Britain, agreeably to a late resolve of the General Court, if in case the wisdom of Congress should see proper to do it."[134] Yarmouth's role in the Revolutionary War represented the efforts of other Nantucket Sound communities: to assist countrymen to the north.

Tourism launched a new era in economic growth for Cape Cod and the Islands, including Englewood Hotel in West Yarmouth. *Courtesy of the Historical Society of Old Yarmouth.*

The year of the American Revolution saw the publication of this 1776 map. *Courtesy of the Norman B. Leventhal Map Center, Boston Public Library.*

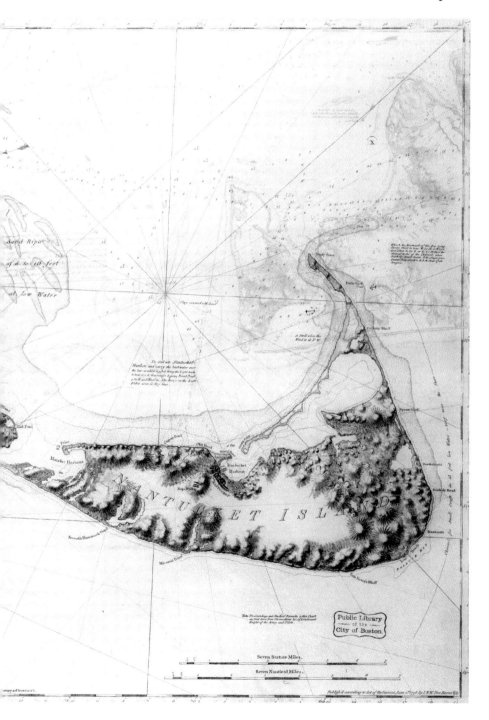

Lewis Bay in Hyannis, now a haven for recreational boaters. *Courtesy of the Historical Society of Old Yarmouth.*

Family and friends gather in Dennis Port in this undated photo. *Courtesy of the Historical Society of Old Yarmouth.*

Harwich sent a contingent of "sea coast guards" to the Elizabeth Islands just west of Nantucket Sound from August 7, 1776, to November 1776, including Solomon Crowell, John Allen and Obediah Eldridge.[135]

For those English warships on patrol in Nantucket Sound for privateers terrorizing citizenry and taking foodstuffs and supplies from towns, they in turn were forced to endure harsh winters. British admiral Samuel Graves said the weather in Cape Cod challenged the most hearty of his sailors: "This sort of storm is so severe that it cannot even be looked against, and By the snow freezing as fast as it falls, baffles all resistance—for the blocks Become choked, the tackle encrusted, the ropes and sails quite congealed, And the whole ship before long one cake of ice."[136]

Following declaration of the beginning of the War of 1812 with Britain, the English sent fleets of warships to the East Coast, and once again Nantucket Sound fisheries came to a standstill for years.

By the time the Civil War broke out, whaling had seen its high-water mark and whaling fleets were downsizing. Southern privateers taunted Yankee merchantmen and whaling and fishing captains at the beginning of hostilities. "Off Hatteras, North Carolina, in early July 1861, the privateer *Winslow* seized the schooner *Herbert Manton* of Centerville, inbound from Cuba with 175 hogshead of sugar and seventy of molasses, Simeon Backus of Osterville her captain," wrote Stauffer Miller in *Hoisting Their Colors: Cape Cod's Civil War Navy Officers*. "A few days later the privateer *Mariner* took her only prize, the schooner *Nathaniel Chase* of Harwich, Daniel Doane of Harwichport the captain, also off North Carolina." The effects of the Union blockade of Southern ports, while designed to starve the Confederacy, had the consequence of ruining the maritime fortunes of New England's coasting captains, recounted historian James J. Coogan Jr.

# Chapter Four

# Fin and Fluke

*I confess I was surprised to find that so many men spent their whole day, ay, their whole lives almost, a-fishing. It is remarkable what a serious business men make of getting their dinners, and how universally shiftlessness and a groveling taste take refuge in a merely ant-like industry. Better go without your dinner, I thought, than be thus everlastingly fishing for it like a cormorant. Of course, viewed from the shore, our pursuits in the country appear not a whit less frivolous.*
—*Henry David Thoreau (1817–1862), from* Cape Cod

*Most wise men on the Cape knew the way to China by sea better than they did the way to Boston by land.*
—*Henry Kittredge*

## Fin

It was 1789 and the unnamed fishing schooner was in desperate trouble in Nantucket Sound.[137] Aboard were its master, Howes Hallet, and six other men, all Yarmouth born and bred: Josiah Hallet, Daniel Hallet, Levi Hallet, Joseph Hallet, Josiah Miller and Moody Sears. The schooner, owned by a Mr. Evans of Providence, Rhode Island, was lost in a gale with all hands.

Fishing was and is dangerous, and the hundreds of wrecked vessels lining Nantucket's sandy floor will attest to that; no blessing of the fleet for these hulks. It was a potentially lethal occupation every day in 1789, as it's dangerous in 2009. The only differences between yesteryear and today are advances in technology such as radar and radio communications.

On October 3, 1841, and into the next day, Captain Eben Bray Jr. had left Nantucket Sound for Georges Bank aboard the schooner *Primrose*. Then the notorious gale swept through, and Bray and his men were not heard from again. In the same storm, four vessels from Dennis were lost, and between those fishing boats, twenty-one boys and men from town perished.[138]

Despite clear dangers, every community on Nantucket Sound sent men and boys to sea to fish; the industry was too lucrative to ignore. Chatham boasted a healthy fishing fleet. Twenty-two vessels were registered in the Chatham fisheries in 1837, and in that year the catch yielded fifteen thousand quintals of cod and 1,200 barrels of mackerel; one quintal equals one hundred pounds.[139]

Historian Burt Derick of South Dennis summarized methods of fishing in Nantucket Sound:

> *Boats from the south shore went out off Martha's Vineyard swordfishing, and some were taken in the Sound. Same for tuna. I know of no locals that did any dragging in the Sound, nor was I aware of any being done before very recently (last 30 years). We always regarded the Sound as a nursery, and one should never mess with the bottom much in summer in a nursery. Much of the grass that washes up on the beaches now is that dislodged by draggers operating out there. The only dragging operations done by local fishermen was done in the fall only. That was before 1944, when the eel-grass beds were destroyed by the hurricane. Those beds produced prodigious amounts of bay scallops. The south shore was also a lucrative place to run liquor during prohibition, very quiet, very shoal where cutters could not go, and many of the locals profited by it during the Depression.*[140]

# Bustling Wharves in Harwich[141]

On May 12, 1879, the *Anna Nash*, a three-masted schooner from Harwich Port, sailed home with its canvas sails whistling in the spring wind and a happy Captain Henry Nickerson hauling a respectable 300 barrels of mackerel in its hold. A day later, the *Crest of the Wave*, under the command of a Captain Melanson of Gloucester, arrived to "take bait" and off it went. Once the *Crest* left the harbor, in came the *Gov. Goodwin* from the South Grounds off Block Island, soon to leave for Portsmouth, New Hampshire, with 420 barrels of mackerel. Right behind the *Gov. Goodwin* was the *Little Lizzie* to offload codfish. Then Captain Freeman Long brought the *Lillie Ernestine* into port to pick up mackerel bound for New York.

Fresh fish was on nearly every supper table in Falmouth, thanks to the Woods Hole Fish Market. *Courtesy of the Falmouth Historical Society.*

The flesh of fish, mainly Cape Cod "turkey," cod and mackerel, nourished fishing families and sustained economies on Nantucket, Martha's Vineyard and Cape Cod for generations.

The 1850 census for Harwich reported that 71 percent of work-eligible men over the age of fifteen were engaged in sea-related trades; this was still a true statistic nearly thirty years later. Harwich boasted five wharves that waded into the shallow waters of Nantucket Sound. Several independent wharves were maintained at Herring River, including Wixon and Baker Wharves. Allen Harbor was not a wharf as we know it but merely an "inside refuge" that opened to Nantucket Sound.

At the center of Harwich Port down Sea Street was Kelley's Wharf, site of a brisk coal and lumber company run by the Kelley brothers. Theophilus B. Baker owned Baker's Wharf at the end of Bank Street, and farther down east was Valentine Doane's Wharf, approximately where the Snow Inn is located. It is widely believed that the wood for the early cottages at Wychmere Harbor came from the remains of Doane's Wharf. Three small wharves were built off Deep Hole Wharf in South Harwich: Commercial, Eldredge and Small Wharves.

At sunrise, ships sailed in and out of the harbor in all directions until sunset. Harwich fishermen worked rich areas within two hundred miles of home: the Grand Banks for codfish and the Gulf of Lawrence and

This proud fisherman hoists a Cape Cod turkey—codfish—ready for market. *Courtesy of the Harwich Historical Society.*

South Grounds off Block Island for mackerel. These prosperous times would not last. Depressions about 1887 and 1893 affected even an isolated Cape Cod and the Islands. Still, through the years, including 1879, Harwich had prospered, and many grew wealthy from the fin-laden gold taken from the sea.

There were risks to this occupation, and dangers were never far from the minds and hearts of families of sea-bound loved ones. While Captain Nickerson was off catching more mackerel, another fishing voyage in May 1879 ended in death for two seamen, blood sons of sea captains who often sent their own boys away to learn the family trade. While in the West Indies aboard the fishing schooner *Hattie M. Hawes*, Chief Mate Emery W. Baker, twenty-five, and the second mate, nineteen-year-old Louis Eldridge, died of yellow fever. No doubt these sons of Harwich were mourned at the Pilgrim Congregational Church on Main Street, whose tall steeple became the famous guidepost for which generations of homeward-bound seamen hungered.

# Pine Grove Seminary

One reason Harwich was among the top fishing communities on Nantucket Sound was a private academy that incorporated a steep curriculum in science and nautical arts. Sidney Brooks was an Amherst-trained teacher who opened Pine Grove Seminary to forty-five students in Harwich Center in December 1844. Doing so cemented Harwich's niche as a nursery of fishermen and mariners even though the academy's curriculum wasn't limited to nautical arts alone. Pine Grove Seminary closed in 1866.

The generous curriculum and ungraded classrooms cost ten dollars a term and offered coursework in literature, math, philosophy and French, complemented by music, art and physical education. The science that Brooks taught was navigation, and this sparked the widespread belief that only seamanship was taught at Pine Grove. The academy's building still stands as the Harwich Historical Society.

Brooks kept a ledger of each student at Pine Grove, but a disgruntled scholar swiped it, so Brooks's official diary was recounted from memory in *Our Village*. In 1866, Sidney Brooks sold the seminary to the town for $1,000 and took a teaching post aboard the state training ship the *George M. Barnard*, "one of the two vessels of about 900 tons each, that comprised the

Nantucket Harbor of yesteryear. *Courtesy of the Nantucket Historical Association.*

Massachusetts Nautical School," he would write later in life. Brooks was later appointed deputy U.S. shipping commissioner in Boston, and died in 1887.

In 1869, quahog beds were discovered near Smith's Point and Tuckernuck, and about June 1872, oysters were planted in Osterville and were expected to pay off handsomely.[142]

If farmers and tradesmen settled Nantucket, it took less than a generation for their ambitions to turn from field to fin. Fishing stages constructed on Nantucket Island were small wooden cabins providing shelter to a fishing crew, on average about five men.[143] Each had a stone fireplace and at least two bedrooms, and enough of these small dwellings were built and were the seed corn for villages, including Quidnet near Nantucket Harbor.[144]

On the afternoon of Thursday, September 14, 1944, Nathaniel Wixon, a weir fisherman from Dennis, sat on a bluff in Dennis Port overlooking his weir in Nantucket Sound, buried his head in his hands and nearly sobbed as a growing and merciless southeast gale destroyed his fishing weir, a sophisticated yet simple series of poles and nets he had meticulously constructed by hand. He peered through binoculars "with tears running down his face, watching his $30,000 investment get torn to hell," said his grandson, Dennis historian Burt Derick. Weir fishing ran in the family: Nathaniel's grandfather, Edgar Wixon, had also set deep-water weirs in 1880 and sold the fish he caught.

Wixon was a hardworking jack-of-all-trades who could fix anything; thrifty, too, he was known to "make any engine run." A middle school in Dennis is named for him. Wixon stopped weir fishing in 1965, but up until then he was firmly committed to the trade. His weirs, according to his grandson and fishing cohort Burt Derick, were on Killpond Bar off Dennis and off Swan River in West Dennis; squid was the primary catch and destined for the white table New York City market. "We *never* ate them," insisted Derick.

For Wixon, the weir fishing season on the Sound lasted from mid-March to the end of May. When summer rolled around, Wixon moved his weirs to Cape Cod Bay, where tuna and mackerel were the chief prizes. Wixon's corps of fishing hands was tightknit and loyal to the boss.[145]

Salting and flaking were the only ways to preserve fish until refrigeration became commonplace in the twentieth century. Today, only a handful of fishermen tend weirs, a network of strategically placed nets where fish swim in but can't get out. Ernie Eldredge and his wife, Shareen Davis, operate several grants in Nantucket Sound.

Bass River was the dividing line between Yarmouth and Dennis, and scores of vessels were built there, and saltworks, too, as well as shellfishing enterprises and piers for numerous fishing vessels.

*Right*: Nathaniel Wixon was a famous weir fisherman from Dennis and a solid community man. A middle school in Dennis bears his name. *Courtesy of Burton N. Derick.*

*Below*: Edgar Wixon kept strict records of his fish business in Dennis, circa 1910. *Courtesy of Burton N. Derick.*

## EDGAR F. WIXON

Dealer in and Shipper of

## All kinds of FRESH FISH.

Telephone Connection 42 - 24. Residence,

"         "         19 - 15. Fish House Herring River, West Harwich, Mass.

DENNIS PORT, MASS., Aug 22 1910

Received of Edgar F. Wixon, Eighty Dollars ($80 00/100) to use in land deal on Herring River.

Louis B.D. Raycroft.

Nathaniel Wixon's employees and friends lived as much on Cape Cod waters as they did on land. This photo by a *Life* magazine photographer was snapped just before World War II but never saw publication. *Left to right*: John Garfield, Stanley Lapham, Charlie West, Clint Cahoon and Red Taylor. *Courtesy of Burton N. Derick.*

Another snapshot of friends and coworkers of Dennis weir fisherman Nathaniel Wixon. *Courtesy of Burton N. Derick.*

A present-day fishing weir in Nantucket Sound replicates weirs of past generations. *Photo by Theresa M. Barbo.*

Bass River shot from West Dennis. Bass River is the longest tidal river in Massachusetts. *Courtesy of the Historical Society of Old Yarmouth.*

# Fluke

*Nothing more happened on the passage worthy the mentioning; so, after a fine run, we safely arrived in Nantucket.*

*Nantucket! Take out your map and look at it. See what a real corner of the world it occupies; how it stands there, away off shore, more lonely than the Eddystone lighthouse. Look at it—a mere hillock, and elbow of sand; all beach, without a background. There is more sand there than you would use in twenty years as a substitute for blotting paper. Some gamesome wights will tell you that they have to plant weeds there, they don't grow naturally; that they import Canada thistles; that they have to send beyond seas for a spile to stop a leak in an oil cask; that pieces of wood in Nantucket are carried about like bits of the true cross in Rome; that people there plant toadstools before their houses, to get under the shade in summer time; that one blade of grass makes an oasis, three blades in a day's walk a prairie; that they wear quicksand shoes, something like Laplander snow-shoes; that they are so shut up, belted about, every way inclosed, surrounded, and made an utter island of by the ocean, that to the very chairs and tables small clams will sometimes be found adhering as to the backs of sea turtles. But these extravaganzas only show that Nantucket is no Illinois.*

—*Herman Melville*, Moby Dick

The first whale men on Nantucket were Native Americans engaged in drift whaling. The first documented one was by 1668, if not sooner.[146] The Wampanoag had jurisdictional rights enforced by deeds to drift whales, as did their white neighbors.[147] In 1672, when most of America was still a wilderness, and indeed, when the continent contained more Native Americans than colonists, the first whale was caught from Nantucket. A year later, shore whaling turned into a small business there. Capitalism reigned since infancy on this tiny spit of an island.

An old yarn on Nantucket claims that in 1690, while on a hill watching whales offshore, one man said to another, "There is a green pasture where our children's grandchildren will go for bread." Something else happened on Nantucket in 1690—a Yarmouth mainland man named Ichabod Paddock went to Nantucket to teach a new seafaring skill: shore whaling. "He taught Nantucket citizens to whale, standardized the whaleboat, and set up shore whaling on Nantucket," according to Cameron Juric, a researcher with the Historical Society of Old Yarmouth.

Nantucket's venerable sage, Obed Macy, himself a whaler, wrote, "The Indians, ever manifesting a disposition for fishing of every kind, readily joined with the whites in this new pursuit, and willingly submitted to any station assigned them. By their assistance, the whites were enabled to fit out and man a far greater number of boats than they could have done of themselves. Nearly every boat was manned in part, many almost entirely, by natives." The industry exploded, and by 1700, shore whaling proved a thriving fishery for Nantucket captains and Native Americans.

The first Nantucket vessel to travel to the South Pacific was the *Beaver*, which sailed there during the summer of 1791, returning in February 1793 with 1,300 barrels of oil. In a letter—made available by the Nantucket Historical Association—to "Mr. E. Raymond" from Frederick C. Sanford, detailing Nantucket's storied whaling history, dated June 13, 1858, it is made clear that Sanford was a pillar of Nantucket society and at one time was president of the Pacific National Bank of Nantucket and historian. Nantucket's glory days of whaling would decline in the 1840s.

"Whereas the *Rebecca*," Sanford continued, "was gone longer and only brought 650 barrels sperm oil. We had 6 ships sail that season." Sanford

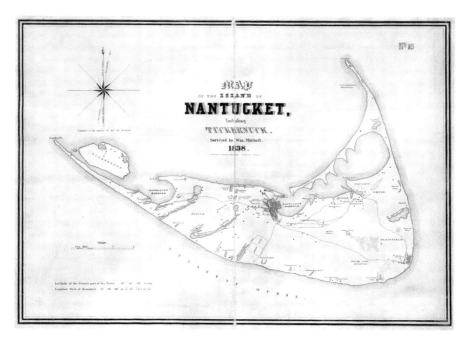

William Mitchell's 1838 map of Nantucket, including Tuckernuck. *Courtesy of the Norman B. Leventhal Map Center, Boston Public Library.*

ended the letter with this other historical fact: "The first whale ever killed in P. Ocean was by a Nantucket man 1788—Archelas Hammond! Who lived next Coffin Whippey's."

An early challenge for whaling entrepreneurs on Nantucket Island was not the raising of capital. An established market and the subsequent demand for goods produced from dead whales proved lucrative.[148] Finding muscle to man whaleboats was the concern. Capitalists were in a quandary given the scarcity of skilled and trustworthy employees. Eventually, the problem would be solved by hiring Native Americans who excelled in whaling. Natives were hired on terms likened to indentured servitude.

In 1712, for the first time, whaling offshore was successful when a sperm whale was killed by a local vessel blown off course in a gale.[149] Several years later, Nantucket whaling captains built tryworks on their ships to process raw products of spermaceti, oil and baleen. Once those materials were home, islanders used baleen as stays in corsets and carved buttons from whalebone.[150] Profits generated from sales of these goods turned into cash money, and wealthier Nantucket residents purchased necessities and luxuries, including furniture, tools and cloth.[151]

From Harwich alone, more than one hundred men were engaged in the "whale fishery."[152] Sailing out of Nantucket Sound, these vessels went as far north as the St. Lawrence River for right whales, so named because they floated when killed and were the "right whales" to hunt for their oil, blubber and baleen. "Among those who commanded whaling vessels here at this period were Edmund Freeman, Joseph Snow, William Gage, Isaac Freeman, Thacher Freeman, Edward Hall, and Lemuel Berry," noted Harwich historian Josiah Paine.

Benjamin Bangs of Harwich noted in his diary the death of Nathan Clarke, "one of the crew of the vessel commanded by Edmund Freeman, who was lost" near the banks of Newfoundland.[153]

Until the Revolutionary War, fishing skippers, whaling masters, coasting captains and merchant mariners prospered, and their professions were often enormously lucrative. There were degrees of wealth, of course, but certainly successful voyages sustained many captains' families and secured their social status.

When war with England broke out in the Bay State, according to Samuel Eliot Morison in his seminal *Maritime History of Massachusetts*, the once invincible fishing fleet took up the cause:

> *In war-time her fishing fleet was dismantled, but the fishermen found exciting employment on armed merchantmen bearing letters of marquee and*

Incomprehensible today, a slaughtered whale is sliced alongside a whaling vessel inside of Nantucket Harbor. *Courtesy of the Nantucket Historical Association.*

*reprisal. A typical Massachusetts-built vessel of the larger class, subject to our unique pre-Revolutionary ship portrait, was the* Bethel, *owned by the Quincy family. Armed with fourteen guns and carrying thirty-eight men, she captured in 1748 by sheer Yankee bluff a Spanish treasure ship of twenty-four guns and one hundred and ten men, "worth the better part of an hundred thousand pounds sterling." So congenial, in fact, did our provincial seamen find privateering, that many could not bear to give it up when peace was concluded. In consequence, not a few were hanged in chains on Bird Island or Nix's mate, whereby every passing seaman might gain a moral lesson.*[154]

An interesting footnote to whaling is the impact the industry had on family life in communities on Nantucket Sound. It was an accepted, common practice for wives to sail with their whaling captain husbands. Over the course of a long marriage, a wife would travel on at least one voyage with her spouse. If she wasn't engaged in handiwork such as knitting or mending, or taking care of children, a Mrs. would not usually socialize or speak to anyone but her husband, the cook and the captain's valet, usually an older boy or the first mate.

Marriage to a whaling captain might mean a long honeymoon off-Cape. "A happy pair were, not long ago, joined in wedlock at Falmouth," noted the *Falmouth Enterprise* in a July 1925 story documenting the heyday of whaling.[155] "Their bridal tour was a whaling voyage that lasted five years. During their absence, the wife gave birth to two babies. One was baptized by a missionary at one of the Society Islands, and was a child of some four years when it reached home. The other was still an infant on arriving at our shores."[156]

Captain and Mrs. Charles H. Turner of Hatchville, a village in Falmouth close to Nantucket Sound, became parents twice over a long whaling voyage. Their Clementine was born in Chile and son Reginald came into the world at St. Helena in the South Atlantic Ocean. In neighboring Teaticket, one village over and just north of Nantucket Sound, Nellie B. Baker, daughter of Nehemiah P. Baker of Teaticket, was born in New Zealand. Procreating on a whale ship certainly ensured the fertility and continuation of the Turner and Baker family lines, as well as large numbers of whaling families on Cape Cod.

For Nantucket women who remained on the island while their husbands sailed the globe in whaling's stellar years from 1800 to about 1850, data suggest a decline in their fertility.[157] From the beginning of its settlement, Nantucket's sandy soil meant that potential traders needed a product with which to engage in business with the mainland.[158] English settlers on Nantucket learned sea trades quickly. From drift whaling to shore whaling to offshore whaling and a rapid succession of skills, whaling expanded to make Nantucket the whaling capital of the world, and after Boston and Salem, the third largest commercial port in Massachusetts.[159] After 1743, when whaling vessels affixed their own tryworks or processing equipment to the vessel, revenues jumped, but so did the length of voyages.[160] While a family's financial ledgers crept upward, the fertility rate on Nantucket declined because husbands were gone for months, or even years, at a time. "A family was considered complete if the marriage remained intact until the wife's forty-fifth birthday or lasted at least 27 years," according to researcher Barbara J. Logue, who studied fertility rates among Nantucket's whaling families. "In incomplete families, on the other hand, the union was disrupted by the death of one spouse prior to the wife's attaining the age of 45," she clarified.[161]

Long absences of husbands, sons, brothers and fathers turned Nantucket into a breeding ground of independent, resourceful women. Having spouses gone for extended periods was an established pattern on Nantucket but virtually unheard of elsewhere in the American countryside except during wartime. On the downside, mothers were turned into de facto single parents living with the ever-present threat of sudden widowhood, given the dangerous nature of whaling.

In his famous *Letters from an American Farmer*, J. Hector St. John de Crevecoeur observed the family patterns on Nantucket:

> *As the sea excursions are often very long, their wives in their absence, are necessarily obliged to transact business, to settle accounts, and in short, to rule and provide for their families. These circumstances being often repeated, give women the abilities as well as a taste for that kind of superintendency, to which, by their prudence and good management, they seem in general to be very equal. This employment ripens their judgement, and justly entitles them to a rank superior to that of other wives; and this is the principal reason why [they] are so fond of society, so affable, and so conversant with the affairs of the world.*[162]

Whaling was a lucrative future to younger, stronger men, so those potential husbands were taken off-Island for years at a time, reducing their chances of marrying and producing children with their wives. Long voyages and short return trips home to Nantucket affected fertility. But as stocks of whale populations were depleted in and around Nantucket Sound, New England and the western North Atlantic, whaling captains extended operations into the Pacific Ocean, increasing their exposure to danger from accident or disease and extending their time at sea.[163]

The most profitable year for sperm oil in the American whaling industry came in 1837, with 5,329,138 gallons; Nantucket whaling captains accounted for part of the take.[164] In 1846, the American whale fishery consisted of 722 vessels valued at nearly $20 million.[165] The most profitable year overall was 1854, when nearly $11 million worth of oil and bone were harvested.[166]

By 1877, the whaling fleet numbered 163 vessels, with New Bedford having the most at 118; Provincetown, 21; Boston, 6; Fairhaven, Marion and Westport—towns near New Bedford—12; New London, Connecticut, 3; and San Francisco, 2.[167] By then, Nantucket's whaling days had ended because large draft ships could not access the shallow harbor.[168] By 1886, forty-nine firms and general agents catered to whaling interests with headquarters at New Bedford and San Francisco.

"The sperm oil catch dropped 50 percent in each of the two decades between 1846 and 1866," writes Arthur R. Railton in *The History of Martha's Vineyard.* "Between 1846 and 1855, it fell from 160,000 barrels to 81,000. In the next decade, it fell to 37,000 barrels. The second decade, of course, was a time of war, and the catch was affected by the destruction of many whale ships by the Confederate raiders *Alabama* and *Shenandoah.* But the decline had started in the 1840s, before the war," clarified Railton.

Overfishing lowered stocks, and it should be pointed out that a silver lining to the Civil War was that it provided a chance for depleted populations of marine mammals to recover some numbers.

# Chapter Five

# SALT, SAIL AND STEAMSHIPS

*Full fathom five thy father lies:*
*Of his bones are coral made:*
*Those are pearls that were his eyes:*
*Nothing of him that doth fade*
*But doth suffer a sea-change*
*Into something rich and strange.*
—*William Shakespeare,* The Tempest

*Dearest Mary again I have attempted to write a line to you knowing your anxiety to hear*
*of my good health and as to that my health is as good as ever it was in my life and I*
*enjoy muyself as well as can be expected considering my being absent from you all I live*
*on Earth Oh, Mary, Deares Mary, it seems to me at this time if ever I am spared to meat*
*with you again that I never shall leave you again.*
—*Captain Henry Manter of Martha's Vineyard in letter to his wife, Mary,*
*October 1844*

The men and boys of Nantucket, Martha's Vineyard and Cape Cod were pioneers who sailed far from their home waters of Nantucket Sound. Without doubt, parallel characteristics were shared with later generations of Americans who boarded covered Conestoga wagons and headed west over ripe prairie grasses; shared principles of self-reliance to ensure survival came into play daily.[169] What was the difference between the canvas atop a covered wagon in the nineteenth century to cross the Indiana territory and the canvas of sails whipping in the wind in the Indian Ocean? Only the locale. Mettle was mettle. Whether on local seas or distant ports did not matter; gone these Nantucket Sound mariners were, like settlers heading west into the midst of plains Indians and unknown elements.[170]

Captain Henry Manter called the village of Holmes Hole on Martha's Vineyard home, shown here in 1865. This village was later known as Vineyard Haven. *Courtesy of the Martha's Vineyard Museum.*

The legends and lore of the men who sailed on and through Nantucket Sound are far grander than the actual humans whose hardships and triumphs inspired those tales, passed on for generations in fishing and merchant families. Behind the quintessential, brave merchant captain or the brawny, fearless sailor were real people, flawed, sensitive, ambitious and often scared.

Hundreds of mothers and fathers sent their boys and young men to sea, close to home waters and distant shores, from every town on Cape Cod, Martha's Vineyard and Nantucket.

Whether a Nantucket whale man gone for months or years, whether a merchant sea captain from Martha's Vineyard or a day fisherman from Harwich, however hearty these seafarers might have been, they were susceptible to human frailties of the heart. They were human, after all, as were the families—the mothers, daughters, wives and younger sons—that were left behind.

Sails in a fury were the order of the day for these schooners in this undated photo on Nantucket Sound. *Courtesy of Detrick Lawrence Productions.*

The dichotomy that intrigues us but was commonplace in their time is the balance of professional challenges and the personal commitments required of captains, who not only displayed absolute power aboard the vessels, but also were loving toward their wives. Not all captains were firm but fair-minded to crew, or faithful and kind to wives and children. Some masters were horrible human beings, but the average master mariner found the balance between work and home to balance the sternness and softness.

About 165 years ago, Captain Henry Manter (1816–1878) put on his black captain's top hat and a jacket and boarded his vessel in Holmes Hole for a long journey. His wife, Mary, began to bear the sorrow of his departure. Though Henry and Mary were formally uneducated, they were brilliant and their penmanship clear and full of the flowery nineteenth-century typical prose, as evidenced in this letter from Mary to Henry:[171]

> *Addressed: Capt Henry Manter, ship* Pocahontas, *Indian and Pacific Ocean*
> *Chilmark, May 17, 1844*

*Ever dearest and much loved Henry,*

*I now improve the first opertunity of writing toyou; I wached you with the glafs until you left the, Packet, and got on board the Ship, sister Robinson staid with us untile night, and then brother Daggett got home and said that you was at anchor in menamesha lite for that night, tell cousin Sylvanus that I went and called his wife, and we went to the vestry, to meeting that evening, and it was a firtrate meeting, and our neace Eeliza, come home with me, and staid all night, and the next morning Capt Richard S. Luce,*

In 1844, Mary Luce Manter wrote love letters to her sea captain husband, Captain Henry Manter, in perfect script. *Courtesy of the Martha's Vineyard Museum.*

*called on me, to know att what time, I wished to leave for Chilmark, James Robinson brought me home that day, and Elisa McDaggett took a ride up with us, and she staid but a short time.*

She went on to say:

*I feel very lonely and lonesome but then I think, I ought not to be when I consider that I am at home with my beloved parents, and can enjoy the society of my friends, but you must try to keep up as good spirits, as possible, and you must endeavour to try to, take all the comfort that you possibly can, knowing that you have, the consolation of Religion to bouy up your sinking spirits in your absence, frome near and dear friends.*

A few months later, Captain Manter wrote to Mary in words and a tone that do not require amplification:

*1844*
*Mrs Henry Manter Holmes Hole M Vineyard Mass*
*A Sea on board Ship* Pocahontas *June 9*

*Dear Mary It is now Sunday Eve and I have been thinking of home the most of the day these days above all the rest causes me to think of you and the*

Vineyard Haven Wharf, 1900. *Courtesy of the Martha's Vineyard Museum.*

*Priviliges I had when with you it greaves me in the heart to think I cannot see you for a long time I know you must miss my company Merry which if it was rather poor I know it was the latter part of my being with you because my hart was troubled within me but I could not help it the dread of being separated from you for so long a time caused me trouble of mind…*

*I have not heard a profane word since I left home I have a good ship and officers and crew as far as I can discover so far but it requires time to asertain that fact.*

Captain Reuben Whelden's schooner was docked at Portsmouth, Virginia, on February 12, 1864, when he composed a quick note to his wife, Susan, in South Dennis, a vibrant maritime village on Nantucket Sound's Cape Cod side. He wrote, "I wish I could clasp you in my arms and give you a good <u>kiss</u>."[172]

Mere slips of paper, these letters to home from hundreds of sea captains, kept the maritime subculture afloat in communities on Nantucket Sound. These letters—tangible evidence of distant love—which arrived in Holmes Hole, Nantucket, Barnstable and all other towns, shipped over months and meridian alike, meant that marriages were sustained via paper and ink. If the marriage was solid then so, too, were families and the towns themselves.

In another letter to wife Susan dated March 20, 1864, off Baltimore, Captain Whelden wrote,

*I suppose it seems an age since you received a letter from your much loved husband…and you are anxious to hear from him, & I am pleased to inform you that we arrived here all safe after quite a long passage from Philada… many times have I though of Dear Wife. To day and as often wished I was with you more than three months have passed since I bid you a good morning And it has seemed as long to me as that. The time is not far distant when we wil have the pleashur of meeting again…I want to see you ever so much.*

A few sentences later, in that same March letter, he wrote to his twenty-nine-year-old wife: "I am loading coal for Providence and I get 9½ cts p Bushel. This is a much better freight then the others," he explains, adding, "we wil take about thirteen Thousand Bushels." Though the correspondence carried the weight of a man's loneliness and angst and in turn a woman's longing for her husband, mail also offered a context for sharing joys and seemingly insignificant happenings.

Captain's Whelden's letters to his wife prove a mix of longing in one sentence, and in the next line he shares the routine worries of a man who wears a captain's hat: "I expect we wil be enloaded the last of next week… anes know where I wil go. I don't get many papers here and ont know where the Vessels are, so you must write me," the captain requests, adding, "I wil write again soon if the weather is good I am going to <u>Norfolk</u> to morrow to mail this and get one from little Wife."

Captain Whelden commanded a coasting vessel, not a deep-sea ship. Susie Baker Whelden would, all through her life, keep the many notes and letters of sympathy she received following the sudden death of Captain Whelden due to a fever in March 1865. All these letters are in the safekeeping of the Dennis Historical Society.

Another Dennis native and slightly younger contemporary of Captain Whelden was Peter H. Crowell, born in April 1837 in West Dennis, the eldest son of Captain Peter Crowell and his wife, Reliance. Young Crowell was close to his father. A good yarn is retold that once Peter refused to take a quarter from his father for work he had done because he felt his "father couldn't afford it."[173]

Crowell died in Florida in March 1923 at the age of eighty-six.[174] The *Yarmouth Register*, in its March 24, 1923 edition, remarked upon the shock of the community that this pillar of the maritime world, who had seen its heyday and its decline, was gone. "When 13 years old he went to sea and at 19 became master of a ship. For thirty years he sailed to all parts of the world, finally retiring to become a member of the ship broking firm of Crowell & Thurlow, with offices at 131 state street. He was also president of the Cape Cod Steamship Company." Captain Crowell, who is buried in West Dennis in a family plot, was survived by his widow, Eunice, three daughters and two sons.[175] Less than a year later, Crowell's former business partner had run the company into bankruptcy.

Seafarers sailing out of Nantucket Sound's ports in yesteryear made their own rules. Laws of the land meant nothing at sea, even though municipal edicts existed in black and white on scrolls at town halls in Holmes Hole on the Vineyard, Mashpee, Chatham and elsewhere in towns bordering Nantucket Sound. Captains ruled oaken decks, with their orders carried out by trusty first mates and down the chain of command. A captain's angry glance, a first mate's furious glare, would send roughened seamen into chills of fear, as you'll soon read. To rule over and manage a floating community of often unruly men on a big wooden ship halfway around the world for months, even years on one voyage, required ironclad, consistent leadership, which was essential to order.

Whaling Captain Uriah Swain of Nantucket, who lived from 1754 to 1810. *Courtesy of the Nantucket Historical Association.*

Off the west coast of South America in 1792, during a war between Spain and Britain, a few Nantucket whale men and seal hunters were caught up in a mild drama between a cruel New London, Connecticut sea captain and his hapless, abused sailor. William Moulton escaped from the schooner *Onico* and its raging master, Captain George Howe.[176] Howe, nearly six feet tall and blind in his right eye, often beat "the Negro cook…unmercifully with his fists," according to Moulton's diary.[177] Near Staten Island, a seal colony and frequent stop for sealskin traders, Moulton fled and made his way across the island to the *Mars*, whose master was the Nantucket whale man and sealskin trader Uriah Swain. Moulton's journey was not easy, and for part of the way he was pursued by Captain Howe, who was armed with a gun.[178] "Climbing almost perpendicular ascents, crossing morasses, dodging under cavelike cliffs, narrowly missing being trapped in landslides, he successes in escaping from his pursuer (who had turned back), and reached Penguin Harbor…here he was kindly received by Captain Swain."[179] [Eight years later, it would be Captain Swain (1754–1810) who would take the *Mars* to China, where he instituted the first commercial transaction between Nantucket and the Far East.][180]

But Moulton's short-lived escape would not last. "A few days later, the *Onico* came around into this harbor and Captain Swain, in accord with the law of the sea, upon demand gave up his runaway to Captain Howe," writes Edouard Stackpole in *The Sea-Hunters.* It would be months later when another opportunity came for Moulton to leave. He had appealed directly to a gathering of ship captains during a court of inquiry held aboard the *Miantonomah* of New London, and won his freedom.[181] Captain Valentine Swain of Nantucket, Uriah's brother, offered a berth to Moulton, but he refused—Moulton instead accepted employment on another Nantucket vessel, the *Favourite*, under a Captain Paddock.[182]

In certainty, fishing and whaling vessels, along with merchant mariners on transglobal commercial routes, were high profile in Nantucket Sound lore. We should not, however, neglect the third arm of the marine workhorse world, the coasting schooners that served as port-to-port transport for goods and people. These vessels, with a relatively war-free era from 1815 to 1860, were outfitted either as water taxis for human commuting or vessels for trading and transporting commercial goods—everything from lumber to coal to food, potatoes and ice.

The historian Henry Kittredge wrote: "The packets sailed from every little creek and harbor alongshore. Such harbors were impossible to vessels of deeper draught; nowhere along the cape, except at Provincetown, was there a harbor fit for sheltering big ships, nor were there any facilities for loading and unloading them."[183] Coastal ports and offshore islands in the Northeast were linked commercially through spry packet vessels of shallow draft or schooners needing the deeper waters of Nantucket Sound, including Bass River.

# The Famous Captain of Martha's Vineyard[184]

Few coasting captains were as colorful or legendary as Captain Zebulon "Zeb" Northrop Tilton of Martha's Vineyard. Zeb was born on December 1, 1866, a sixth-generation Vineyarder who had six brothers and one sister, all of whom had red hair except for the brunette Zeb.

Zeb signed onto coastal packet work in 1882 at age fifteen aboard the schooner *Eliza Jane*, a trim two-master with forty tonnage, working for Captain Josiah Cleveland, who would become Zeb's mentor. Cleveland was meticulous, honest, fair and thoroughly strict beyond measure. He never wasted time and was known to hand weave eel pots from oak strips and scrub pine roots with meticulous care. The crew included Captain Cleveland's son, Ben Franklin Cleveland, who served as mate.

The walk to the dock at Vineyard Haven from Zeb's home was a good ten miles, but Zeb was unfazed by the distance. Indeed, nothing much bothered

Captain Zeb Tilton at the wheel of the *Wentworth*. *Courtesy of Detrick Lawrence Productions.*

Tilton. Zeb's charm, generosity toward family and friends, keen sense of humor and confidence in the world about him were factors that made him attractive to be around.

Tall and lean, with long, broad arms, Zeb was an incredibly strong, agile man with roughened hands, size fourteen boots and a face that had seen milder days. Zeb Tilton was not handsome in a conventional manner. He was born with crossed eyes that he joked about later in life: "I got the advantage; I can see both ways at once." He was solid through and through, one huge guy, and sturdy, too, like an oak tree. He was quick and strong—all strength and speed. Tilton had a voice that boomed with song—all his siblings sang, save his sister Flora—and Zeb's harmonies carried over the salt marshes and the Vineyard landscape. On a windless day, his verses were heard a half mile off.

After working for Captain Cleveland for eighteen years, Zeb felt a need to strike out on his own and purchased the sixty-tonnage, aging Vineyard Haven two-master *Wilfred J. Fuller* in 1900. Once he spruced up the vessel, business was booming. "He never bothered with a chart but had, instead, memorized the location of every ledge and shoal during his years with Cleveland," wrote historian Polly Burroughs. Tilton relied solely on a compass, and if he got into trouble, there was always a lead line. "This instrument was simply a cylindrical piece of lead, cupped at one end with an eye on the other to attach a line. When it was dropped overboard and sank to the bottom, Zeb could measure both the water's depth and verify his location by the color and quality of the sand or mud which he found in the cup after it was retrieved," recounted Burroughs.

Zeb liked a clean but full galley and often had hot gingerbread, biscuits and a pot of stew on the stove.

Tilton adored women, and they loved him. Perhaps it was the way he had full command of his vessel, his confident manner and what he said to charm them, but the girls wanted Zeb, and badly, despite his crossed eyes and homely face. Zeb had a special something. He married three times. The first Mrs. Tilton was a Vineyard girl, Grace Cook, a flirt known as a "sultry lass." Zeb was twenty-eight and Grace was nineteen when they married in Vineyard Haven in 1894. The marriage lasted only two years; Zeb eventually returned home to find Grace entertaining other men, and they soon divorced. In 1901, a year after he had bought the *Fuller*, Zeb married for a second time to another Vineyard girl, and this time the marriage lasted. When shy Edith

The bow of the schooner *Wentworth*, one of Martha's Vineyard's most celebrated vessels. *Courtesy of Detrick Lawrence Productions.*

Mayhew, a descendant of the island's founders, wed Zeb Tilton, also from an established clan, "two founding families were united in Cottage City," says Burroughs. Together Zeb and Edith raised a family of ten children. They were married until Edith's death in April 1936. For the most part, their marriage was happy, but Zeb's crossed eyes wandered.

In his work life, Zeb's services were in high demand, and he hauled everything, from coal to bricks to clay to ice, busily aboard the *Fuller*. But in 1906, in Portland's harbor, Zeb's apple cart toppled when he got a glimpse of the gal who would steal his soul, the only female to whom he gave his entire heart: the schooner *Alice S. Wentworth*.

Seventy-three feet long with a broad beam and a draw of only five and a half feet—seven and a half when full—the *Alice S. Wentworth* came with a spacious cabin and when fully loaded could haul upward of one hundred tons. It was owned by Captain Charles Stevens and named for the captain's

Loading coal on Martha's Vineyard on the schooner *Wentworth*. *Courtesy of Detrick Lawrence Productions.*

favorite niece. Eventually, Zeb purchased the *Wentworth* from Captain Stevens for $4,500, fifteen years after he first laid eyes on it in Maine. By now, Captain Tilton was fifty-four. Within years, Zeb's fame grew. Zeb sailed through the 1930s, and he'd often stop in Nantucket to host deck parties with music, dancing and food. The actor James Cagney sailed with Zeb once. The quintessential Yankee, Tilton attracted attention wherever he sailed, and he hauled every and any commodity that required transport, even coal.

Zeb's mounting debts forced the U.S. marshal to seize the *Wentworth* on January 15, 1939. Eighteen years of a love affair were apparently over. But at the public auction to sell the vessel, Zeb's friends each bought shares, making it possible that Zeb would sail once again under a cooperative venture in which he was now an employee and "just" a captain. But he didn't mind; he and his beloved *Alice* were again reunited.

Now in his seventies, Zeb still sailed the *Wentworth*, the "last commercial cargo carrier under sail in southern New England," Burroughs said. Another gal caught his eye: the portly but gentle Grace McDonald from New Bedford. After a long courtship haunted by the press—for Zeb was a famous man by this time—she and Zeb married on Saturday, January 13, 1940, in Vineyard Haven. They were married until Grace's death in 1948; she had been ill for seven of their years together. Zeb died of cancer at the age of eighty-five on February 28, 1952, the night a vicious nor'easter blew through New England.

# Steamships

The engines of the 9:15 a.m. Steamship Authority Ferry from Woods Hole to Martha's Vineyard thunder through the gray waves on this chilly early spring morning. The vessel is filled, not to capacity, but enough to see a range of people milling about. A construction crew huddles over coffee, and I hear their voices above the din of the engines. Two retired couples with cameras around their necks eagerly anticipate a trip to the Vineyard. There must be at least one hundred people on the ferry with me.

As we motor into Vineyard Haven, rooftops of antique homes appear alongside the clapboard and shingles of contemporary residences. An outbound vessel, a truck ferry, the *Gay Head*, lies to our port.

The only difference between this ferry and the first ever steamship in Nantucket Sound in the nineteenth century is technological advance. Yesteryear, steam ruled. Diesel engines are king in these times. The constant and common denominator, however, is safety and the efficient shuttle of passengers and cargo, even mail, between the islands and the mainland.

The inaugural trip in a steamship on Nantucket Sound, indeed any vessel using steam, was on May 5, 1818, aboard the *Eagle*, an eighty-ton vessel built in New London, Connecticut.[185] At ninety-two feet long, it carried about sixty passengers on that first trip and revolutionized the way residents and visitors leave the mainland for Nantucket or Martha's Vineyard. To the *Eagle* goes another accolade: it was the first vessel to tow another vessel into Nantucket Harbor under steam. The whale ship *George* was returning from a Pacific Ocean voyage in July 1818 with over two thousand barrels of sperm oil in its hold. The *Eagle*'s historic tenure was short-lived. Growing costs and low ridership ended its reign in the Sound after three months. But the idea, the concept of steam on the Sound, had launched a new maritime industry and mode of travel. Mapmakers began including steamship routes on their documents.

Each steamship has its history. One of the earliest side-wheel ferries was the *Marco Bozzaris*, named by Captain Jacob Barker, a remarkably talented visionary and businessman who was a conduit between the federal government and Nantucket bankers during downturns in the economy.[186] The *Marco Bozzaris* was named for a poem that one of Barker's employees, Fitz-Greene Halleck, was writing. "Oh, just a few stanzas," Halleck, who would later become a famous poet, replied. Barker asked for a reading, and Halleck recited the following:

Water around a steamer freezes in Nantucket Sound. *Courtesy of the Nantucket Historical Association.*

Ferry service to the Islands revolutionized passenger travel in Nantucket Sound. *Painting of the Martha's Vineyard Steamship by William R. Davis. Courtesy of Susan and DeWitt Davenport, Bass River.*

*Marco Bozzaris*
*At midnight, in his guarded tent,*
*The Turk was dreaming of the hour*
*When Greece, her knee in suppliance bent,*
*Should tremble at his power.*

Inspired, Barker took the name of the poem for "my little steamer," all 140 tons of it.[187] In April 1829, the *Marco Bozzaris* made its first trip across the Sound on the Nantucket to New Bedford run.

Steamship service in Nantucket Sound began as an individual enterprise or among small groups of maritime businessmen.[188] The first operating company was the Nantucket Steamboat Company, which later became the Nantucket and Cape Cod Steamboat Company. Between 1848 and 1949, no fewer than ten other companies operated steamship service between Woods Hole and all or some of Cape Cod, Martha's Vineyard and Nantucket, with Woods Hole, Hyannis and New Bedford part of some or all transit routes. At least forty steamships have sailed for various firms.[189] Some were wrecked while on duty, including the *Nantucket*, which operated from 1886 to 1910, from Woods Hole to Nantucket. Before the *Nantucket* was the *Massachusetts*, in service from 1832 to 1842, on a route from New Bedford, Woods Hole,

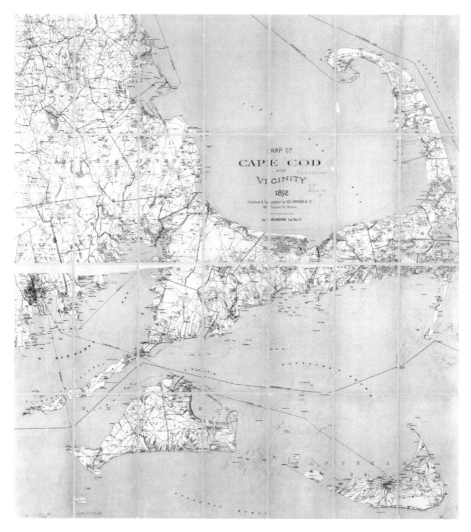

This 1892 map could be taken out of a contemporary map book for its clarity and accuracy. Look closely at the steamship ferry routes marked in black ink that crisscross Buzzards Bay, Vineyard Haven and into Nantucket Sound. *Courtesy of the Norman B. Leventhal Map Center, Boston Public Library.*

Martha's Vineyard and then to Nantucket.[190] After years of faithful service, its owners had it sold for scrap.

In the July 10, 1830 edition of the *Nantucket Inquirer*, a reporter recounted the first steamboat trip from Boston to Nantucket aboard the *Chancellor Livingston*, on which three hundred paying pleasure seekers were living large for a day.[191] When nearing Nantucket, the *Livingston* hit a sandbar and got stuck, but for a fee of forty dollars, Captain Barker used the *Marco Bozzaris* to ferry passengers to the island and returned them later that evening.[192] "It was a matter of regret to thousands that the *Chancellor Livingston* could not pass the bar and visit the inner harbor, and lie a few hours at the wharf, that the curiosity of the citizens generally might be gratified by viewing what, half a century ago, would have astonished the world."[193]

Steamships revolutionized the way Nantucket Sound residents used the ecosystem for travel, pleasure and commercial gain. These vessels changed the tempo of human uses in the Sound, ushering in a new era of ensuring the safety of mariners and the general public who traverse the water sheet. The technology provided seed corn for the growing staple crop of tourists who flocked to mainland and island seaside resorts, including the Harbor View Hotel in Edgartown, which was packed with summer tourists in August 1896.[194]

Nantucket Sound was like a giant city on water filled with people going to work, commuting or taking a vacation. And keeping them safe grew into a paramount concern.

# Chapter Six

# Lighthouses, Lightships and Lifesavers

*The beauty of the soul shines out when a man bears with composure one heavy mischance after another, not because he does not feel them, but because he is a man of high and heroic temper.*
*—Aristotle (384–322 BC)*

On January 31, 1881, from his home in West Dennis, along the shores of Nantucket Sound, Captain William Garfield composed a letter to his distant cousin, President James A. Garfield, imploring the commander in chief to please resurrect the West Dennis Lighthouse. Captain Garfield was concerned that his vessel, "a thousand tons Register," would wreck without this aid to navigation.[195]

*With Coal the freight Bisness is gitting So Poor that a vessel under a thousand tons Cant Do anything So General i Shall drop you a Line or too a gain on account of a Light House We Have Here that Has Bin Standing for twenty five years and Last October it Was put out By the Light Hous Board We Have Sent in a Large Petition for them to Re Light it a gain our Harbor is one of the best that there is in the Vinyard Sound all vessel Come in Here in Bad Weather and no Light it makes it Bad for Large vessel When you git in Washington and git evry thing Werking Well then We Shall Write you and Se if you Can do any thing for this Light House So Remain yours Respetfully*

*William Garfield*
*West Dennis*
*Mass.*

The lighthouse was eventually reopened on July 1, 1881.

Nantucket Sound's convenience as a maritime shortcut from Boston to New York and southern ports came with a price: the shallow Sound was a watery maze of dynamic shoals and even shallower bars that only an experienced pilot or captain could sail safely. One sailed at his own risk.

By the middle of the eighteenth century and well into the nineteenth and twentieth centuries, most of the descendants of the Sound's first English farming settlers went to sea or worked land-based maritime trades. Nantucket Sound was a defined route, and keeping seagoing mariners and their vessels safe became a priority for a marine commercial culture.

# Lighthouses

The first type of aid to navigation to shepherd vessels to shore and orient them at sea was the lighthouse. Of the forty-four lighthouses built in Massachusetts between 1746 and 1961, thirty-nine were in the waters off Cape Cod, Martha's Vineyard, Vineyard Sound and Buzzards Bay, and this included waters south of the Vineyard and Nantucket.[196]

Nantucket's Brant Point Lighthouse, constructed at the harbor's entrance in 1746, was the first in the Sound. It was a simple structure—a short wooden tower topped with a beacon. The Great Point Lighthouse on the northern tip of Nantucket was built in 1784 and greatly added to mariners' comfort as a marker once the Pollock Rip Shoal was passed.

With a range of nine miles, the Cape Pogue Lighthouse was built on Chappaquiddick Island on the eastern side of Martha's Vineyard in 1801. The eastern edge of Nantucket Sound was guided by the Chatham Harbor Lighthouse, which was constructed in 1808 with a range of twenty-eight miles.

Other lighthouses in Nantucket Sound proper were Point Gammon on Great Island in West Yarmouth (1816); West Chop in Vineyard Haven on Martha's Vineyard (1818); Monomoy Point on Monomoy Island in Chatham (1823); Edgartown Harbor Lighthouse on Martha's Vineyard (1828); Nobska Lighthouse in Woods Hole (1829); and Hyannis Harbor (1829).

With a range of eight miles, the South Hyannis Lighthouse is in Hyannis Port and was finished in 1849. Now known as the Lighthouse Inn in West Dennis, the Bass River Lighthouse was completed in 1855 and had a range of twelve miles. South of Point Gammon, and finished in 1858, the Bishop and Clerks Lighthouse once flashed a white light for thirteen miles; these days, with only its base of rock left and with the lighthouse no longer standing, it's actually a hazard to navigation.

Now long gone, the former Bishop and Clerks Lighthouse guided mariners near Bass River in South Yarmouth. *Painting by William R. Davis. Courtesy of Susan and DeWitt Davenport, Bass River.*

Three other lighthouses were built in Nantucket Sound: Hyannis Wharf Range in Hyannis Harbor (1872); East Chop in Oak Bluffs on Martha's Vineyard (1872); and Stage Harbor in Chatham (1880).

As a duty station, lighthouse work was isolating and relatively easy but repetitive. Asa L. Jones, a Harwich native, was keeper from 1875 to 1886 at Monomoy, located just within an arm's reach of Nantucket Sound. The keeper's house and the state-of-the-art, forty-foot cast-iron lighthouse were rebuilt in 1849 on the original location established in 1823, located at Monomoy's southern end. A fourth-order Fresnel lens was brought in 1857, one with the power and brightness of twenty-five thousand candles. The lens on a Fresnel allowed lighthouses to cast a brighter light over longer distances.

The Monomoy Point Light Station was deactivated in 1923, and today the U.S. Fish and Wildlife Service operates the area as the Monomoy National Wildlife Refuge.

# Lightships

The first lightships were active in New England waters in 1820 and were managed by the United States Light House Establishment, later the United States Lighthouse Service. Lightships were part of the U.S. navigation roadmap; think of them as sea-based lighthouses.[197] A lightship "station" was nothing more than a specific point at sea—located by latitude and longitude—positioned at dangerous locations to warn ships to stay clear by the use of flashing lights, and blasting a foghorn about 2,800 times every twenty-four hours, and by radio beacon. Early generations were constructed of wood, with copper and iron fastenings, and sailors used a hand-operated bell, lanterns and oil lamps as warning beacons. Later in the twentieth century, lightship manufacturers replaced wood with steel.

By 1864, thirteen lightships guarded New England's coastline. In Nantucket Sound there were five lightships: *Succonnesset* (1854–1912); *Hedge Fence* (1908–33); *Bishop and Clerks* (1855–58); *Cross Rip* (1828–1964); and *Handkerchief* (1858–1951).

To the west, at the southern tip of the Elizabeth Islands, the famous Vineyard Sound lightship saw duty from 1847 to 1961. To its north was the *Hen(s) and Chickens* lightship (1866–1954). While those two are not in the boundaries of Nantucket Sound, they are certainly part of the Cape Cod family of lightships. Past Monomoy, just outside the Sound and probably within shouting distance, were three lightships: *Stonehorse* (1919–63); *Shovelful Shoal* (1852–1916); and the second location for the *Stonehorse* (1916–19).

The lightship *Cross Rip* is one of seven vessels to bear that name.
*Courtesy of the late WO Bernard C. Webber (Ret.).*

And farther east outside the Sound but within the local lightship family were others: *Pollock Rip Shoals* (1902–23); and three vessels that bore the same name, *Pollock Rip*, but were actually stationed in three different, but close, areas—*Pollock Rip* (1849–1923), which was moved to the northeast from 1923 until 1926, and from 1926 until 1969 in its final position before it was decommissioned. The southernmost lightship was the *Great Round Shoals* (1890–1932).

All lightship locations were serviced by various ships with the same name though different numbers. When undergoing repairs, a clearly marked RELIEF lightship took up a temporary post.

The first lightship on Nantucket Sound designed to warn mariners of a shallow shoal came on station on June 30, 1828, and carried a 750-pound bow anchor and a 1,300-pound iron mushroom anchor. Captain Henry Barnard estimated that about fourteen thousand vessels sailed by the lightship in its first year. It was called, simply, the Tuckernuck Floating Light Boat. A few years later, that same unnamed vessel was moved to the Cross Rip Shoal, garnering not only a permanent location but a new name.

The sixth lightship to stand watch over the notorious Cross Rip Shoal north of Nantucket was frozen in, packed in ice in deep winter of 1917–18. Three other lightships were also frozen in during that infamous arcticlike wedge of ice in the Sound, but two managed to escape and the third "was dragged to Long Island before the crew was saved," according to historian Frederick L. Thompson.

The fate of the fourth lightship, the *Cross Rip*, wasn't as fortunate. On February 1, 1918, the ice sheet was on the move, and the old Lightship #6 "parted its riding gear," according to Harwich harbormaster Tom Leach. Four days later, the keeper of the Great Point Lighthouse, east of the *Great Round Shoal* Lightship Station, saw the *Cross Rip*, bound due east, within the grasp of the ice sheet. The crew was never heard from again. All hands were lost: Frank Johnson, machinist, South Yarmouth; Henry Joy, first mate, Dennis Port; William Rose, cook, North Harwich; Almond Wixon, seaman, Dennis Port; Arthur C. Joy, seaman, Dennis Port; and E.H. Phillips, seaman, West Dennis, according to Leach's article, "Lightships of Nantucket Sound."

In 1939, the Coast Guard took over the U.S. Lighthouse Service and all aids to navigation, such as rules and regulations, charts and placement of buoys. In 163 years, 179 lightships manned 116 "stations," or spots in the ocean where they lay at anchor. In 163 years of service, about 50 lightship sailors have died in the line of duty. The Coast Guard discontinued its lightship service in 1989.

As a young man, the Reverend Dan Davidson of West Yarmouth was a chief engineman who served on the *Cross Rip* until it was decommissioned in January 1954. "It was one of the cleanest ships I was on," remembered the seventy-four-year-old. "To keep busy, we polished and the brass in the engine room was clean, clean, clean. It could be a boring life, because you had to make yourself busy, and if you didn't you would go out of your gourd." Davidson, now the associate pastor at the First Congregational Church in Yarmouth Port, said that every week a small Coast Guard vessel would deliver food, supplies and mail to the *Cross Rip*, and transfer personnel as needed. He added that the first lightships were "manned by prisoners from the Barnstable jail."

In 2007, George E. Rongner self-published his memoirs, *Life Aboard a Coast Guard Lightship*, and said that eating a meal during a storm was a job in itself. "Rubber mats kept the tablecloth from becoming a veritable skating rink, so the problem of keeping food from sliding off was not acute…the men had to sit with their feet braced against the motion of the ship." A wonderful exhibit about Cape Cod and Nantucket Sound lightships is at the Coast Guard Heritage Museum at the Trayser in Barnstable, led by its dedicated executive director, William Collette, himself a veteran lightship man.

# Lifesavers

On January 5, 1786, over lunch at the famous Bunch of Grapes tavern on State Street in Boston, a group of men, many of whom had fought in the American Revolution, founded the Humane Society of the Commonwealth of Massachusetts.[198] The society's goal was to rescue people whose lives were threatened by shipwrecks and drowning. The concept for the Massachusetts Humane Society (MHS) came from an English model, the newly formed British Humane Society, which was inaugurated in 1774. Massachusetts governor James Bowdoin, also founder of Bowdoin College, was elected the first president.

An awards system was set up by the MHS, with funds raised through subscription, to recognize citizen lifesavers. An early subscriber was Paul Revere. The first recipient was Andrew Sloane, who saved a boy in Mill Dam. Gold medals would also be part of the awards system, and the first went to a Lieutenant Scott who jumped from a ship into Boston Harbor and saved a young boy's life. Scott's gold medal cost "two pounds, twelve shillings, eight pence," and would be the first of over 3,700 awards that trustees would distribute over the next two hundred years.

A second phase of the Massachusetts Humane Society was to shelter shipwrecked or stranded mariners in "Huts of Refuge." In 1787, three were constructed in Boston Harbor and south of Boston at Nantasket and Scituate. Maurice Gibbs is a retired navy commander and president emeritus of the Nantucket Shipwreck & Lifesaving Museum. He confirmed that the first U.S. Life-Saving Service (USLSS) station on Nantucket was at Surfside in 1874, but not on the Sound side. The first USLSS stations on Nantucket Sound were at Muskeget Island, part of Nantucket County, and Coskata, at the base of Great Point, in 1883, and in 1890, at Great Neck, later known as Madaket. In 1807, the Massachusetts Humane Society began active rescue work and the trustees ordered construction of lifeboats. Nantucket whale man William Raymond was commissioned to build the first lifeboat, modeled after a British lifeboat, made with cork flotation and designed for a crew of ten lifesavers. Numerous others were sited on the Cape's Outer Shore, outside of the Sound.

"The secret of the success of the MHS was its strong board of trustees in Boston and their system of creating local committees at each coastal town that answered to the board," clarified Gibbs. "These volunteer stations of the MHS functioned until the mid-1930s, the last being closed in 1936."

At the federal level, on August 4, 1790, President George Washington signed legislation authorizing the construction of ten cutters to collect duty and act as security for the port cities of fledgling America. It was originally known as "a system of cutters." This is the date that the Coast Guard celebrates as its birthday. Alexander Hamilton served as the first secretary of the treasury, which oversaw the operation of these cutters. The burgeoning service was also known as the Revenue-Marine, and this service enforced customs laws.

By August 1848, Congress had appropriated funds for lifesaving equipment along New Jersey's shore. "While the Massachusetts Humane Society was the model for much that would follow in the federal system, the creation of stations along the New Jersey and Long Island coasts would ultimately prove only partially successful due to a lack of leadership that was so evident in the success of the MHS," Gibbs clarified.

In 1852, the Lighthouse Service evolved from the former U.S. Lighthouse Establishment with a new board to oversee these aids to navigation. Gibbs added that Congress forced an assessment of the inefficiencies of the original Lighthouse Establishment and reorganized it into the new name—the U.S. Lighthouse Service—in 1852, with a strong board of overseers.

George Sewall Boutwell (1818–1905) was born in Brookline, Massachusetts, and the measure of his legacy would influence marine safety on Nantucket Sound and indeed, across the American coastline.[199] After eight years in the Massachusetts legislature, Boutwell won elections as governor of the Commonwealth of Massachusetts in 1850 and 1852.[200] President Abraham Lincoln appointed Boutwell as the first commissioner of the internal revenue until 1863, when he was elected to Congress as the Civil War was flaring. He served four terms until 1869.[201] The year Boutwell left Congress, in 1869, President Ulysses S. Grant handpicked Boutwell for treasury secretary.

Boutwell launched an "executive search" for a professional to reform the bureau, "its cutters having become little more than the pleasure yachts of public men."[202] He chose Sumner Increase Kimball, a thirty-six-year-old former Maine legislator and lawyer who was employed as chief clerk in the treasury's second auditor's office. Boutwell offered the post of superintendent but Kimball took a week to accept, and with one caveat:

> *Mr. Secretary, I shall accept your offer upon one condition. If you will stand by me, after I have convinced you that I am right, I shall attempt to*

Sumner Increase Kimball (1834–1923) organized the United States Life-Saving Service. *Courtesy of William Collette, Coast Guard Heritage Museum at the Trayser.*

*bring about the reforms you desire. But I want to warn you that the pressure will be tremendous. Congressmen will come to you in long processions and will attempt to convince you that I am wrong and that the service is being ruined. It will require an uncommon display of backbone on your part, but if you will stand firm and refer all complaints to me I promise you that I shall put the service where you want it and where it ought to be.*[203]

Boutwell did not wince and accepted Kimball's terms. "I shall support you. No matter what the pressure may be, I shall not interfere."[204]

Gibbs explained,

*In 1871, Kimball rejuvenated the U.S. Life-Saving Service, which had all but withered away since its inception in 1848. Kimball assumed the position of chief of the Department of Revenue Marine Division. This included the Revenue Cutter Service, Steamboat Inspection Service, Lighthouse Service…It was in a reorganized treasury that the U.S. Life-Saving Service was established as a separate agency in 1878, and Kimball was able to consolidate his direction over the service.*

Kimball would stay in government service for the next forty-four years.

# Cape Cod Lifesavers

Captain William T. Tuttle of Harwich was the tall, bearded and brave lifesaver in charge of the Monomoy Life-Saving Station from 1882 to 1899. During those years, Tuttle led a six-man crew and saved the crew of the foundering schooner *Ellen Morrison*, carrying a cargo of lumber from Maine bound for New London in a northwest gale.

The storm forced the schooner into Chatham for the night, but as the vessel headed toward Pollock Rip a southwest gale kicked up, and the *Morrison* captain said that "her seams must have opened, for she began to leak so fast that our pumps were useless, and the vessel became so loggy that she would not come to stays."[205] Slowly the vessel was ripped apart, "leaving our vessel unmanageable in the trough of the sea, and drifting helplessly toward the breakers under our lee," added the captain, as told to a *Boston Globe* reporter.[206] Before the *Ellen Morrison* sank, Captain Tuttle and his crew arrived. They were exhausted from rowing for two hours against the storm and wet to the core, but they were there.

"And then with consummate skill, Capt Tuttle and his experienced men shot up alongside on the crest of great waves, and took off the sailors one by one, until all were in the lifeboat, and then squared away before the gale

Captain Richard Tuttle of Harwich Port commanded the Monomoy Life-Saving Service Station from 1882 to 1899.
*Courtesy of the Harwich Historical Society.*

toward the shore they had left three hours before," reported the undated *Globe* article at the Harwich Historical Society, donated by a Tuttle ancestor who neglected to include the date.

Tuttle was respected in the community and loved by his men. He died suddenly at home, at age fifty, on Sunday, July 2, 1899. The *Harwich Independent* says that the cause of death was "due to exposure while crossing in his boat from Harwich Port to Monomoy during the severe thunder storm of June 24th. His sickness early developed into typhoid fever and death came in a week after he was taken."[207] His grandson, William Truman Tuttle, however, said that Captain Tuttle's illness was contracted through drinking contaminated water on Cuttyhunk Island, past the western border of Nantucket Sound.

However Captain Tuttle died, the Life-Saving Service lost a respected and apt leader:

> *It is currently reported that Capt. Tuttle has probably landed more men from distressed vessels in life boats than any other keeper. He enjoyed the unlimited confidence of those highest in authority of the department, and no great storm occurred on the coast that his name was not heralded abroad in connection with some perilous adventure of himself and crew. He never counted the cost to himself personally, not even his life, but saw only his duty in times of peril to vessels and crews. He knew no danger, he saw no unsurmountable obstacles, but to act and that promptly and fearlessly as a saviour of his fellow men, was his mission, and in that he made a record that shines with the luster of gold and as a monument to the efficiency of the life saving service. His characteristics were courage, honesty and loyalty to duty.[208]*

Tuttle was survived by his widow, the former Estelle Norwood of Biddeford, Maine, and two children, Olive Estelle, seventeen, and James Norwood, fourteen.[209] His funeral in Harwich Port on July 4, 1899, was widely attended, and pallbearers were Tuttle's men, except for Richard Gage from the Orleans Station, and included "Messrs. S. Linwood Ellis, Thomas Foy, Osborn Chase, Valentine D. Nickerson, Marshal Eldridge," according to the *Harwich Independent*. All proudly wore Life-Saving Service uniforms.

On January 28, 1915, President Woodrow Wilson signed an act into law creating the United States Coast Guard, which merged the U.S. Revenue Cutter Service with the U.S. Life-Saving Service. On June 30, 1932, the U.S. Steamboat Inspection Service and the Bureau of Navigation were merged under the umbrella of the Commerce Department. Seven years later, on July 1, 1939, the U.S. Lighthouse Service merged with the United

States Coast Guard; oversight of all lightships and lighthouses fell to the Coast Guard. In addition, all aids to navigation, including buoys, buoy placement and maintenance, rules, regulations and charts, also reverted to the Coast Guard.

For the duration of World War II, the Coast Guard was transferred to the Department of the Navy but was returned to the control of the Treasury Department on January 1, 1946. The U.S. Steamboat Inspection Service and the Bureau of Navigation came under Coast Guard control by the mid-1940s. In 1967, the Coast Guard's federal oversight agency moved from the Treasury Department to the newly formed Department of Transportation; since 2002, the Coast Guard has been overseen by the Department of Homeland Security.[210]

In Nantucket Sound, the Coast Guard is attached to Sector Southeast New England, with headquarters in Woods Hole. The Coast Guard station on Martha's Vineyard is in Menemsha, to the southwest of the island outside Nantucket Sound. Nantucket is served by the Coast Guard station at Brant Point, and of course, there's another large station at Coast Guard Sector headquarters called Coast Guard Station Woods Hole. Coast Guard Station Chatham is on the other side of Monomoy, but Coast Guard vessels in Stage Harbor service Nantucket Sound.

Captain W. Russell Webster (Ret.) knows Nantucket Sound well, having served as group commander from 1998 to 2001. Webster offered reflections of Nantucket Sound:

> *I knew Nantucket Sound's storied past and made sure my modern-day crews were the best led, best trained, best equipped crews anywhere. The seas and the weather could and did change at a moment's notice. Fog was always a threat in summer. Rescue stations that operated on the Sound were frequently the test beds for new, more capable boats and rescue techniques, understanding that crews here were challenged on a daily basis. The Chatham Rescue Station was the only of my nine stations to require professional "surfmen" who had enhanced, more rigorous training protocols. They needed it, given the bar's shifting sands and dangerous conditions that changed minute by minute. Navigation buoys here were just rough guidelines and no assurance that yesterday's marked channel was today's safe passage. Chatham alone required two launch points for its four rescue boats and, in my three short years, used seven different boats of different varieties to address the vagaries of the environment.*[211]

\*\*

Bernard C. Webber, who retired as a Coast Guard warrant officer in 1966, died of a heart attack in January 2009 at the age of eighty-one at his home in Florida. He spent over twenty years in the Coast Guard (1946–66), with many years in Cape Cod waters. Bernie knew Nantucket Sound well. Before his death, Bernie shared a private memoir of working for the Coast Guard in the Sound:

*The Captain Has the Last Word*
*By: WO Bernard C. Webber (USCG Ret.)*

*I requested a transfer from the Coast Guard Cutter* White Sage *based at Woods Hole to the presidential security patrol at Hyannis. Through the "grapevine" I heard there was a good chance the transfer would be approved. The Captain of the* White Sage *hailed from the Deep South and his disdain for "Yankees" was obvious. I was about as Yankee as one could be and the Captain at every opportunity took advantage of the fact by taunting me. One day orders came through transferring me to the*

In this undated photo, an earlier generation of the Coast Guard is in flight over Nantucket Sound. *Courtesy of the Falmouth Historical Society.*

*Presidential Security Patrol, exactly as I had requested. It would be two weeks before I was to report, the Captain clearly made it known to me, and it would be two weeks I would never forget. I continued to serve my time on board* White Sage *with difficulty and remained calm and aloof which irked the Captain even more as he would continue to taunt me. The day finally came when I was to pack my bags and depart the ship. As I did so and picked up my orders and was about to depart the ship saying my goodbye's to members of the crew, I heard a familiar voice say, "Hey, Chief, ya'all better hold up down-theah, don't make to speedy a depart'cha, son, ya'heah." It was the voice of the Captain up on the ship's bridge talking to me through the pilothouse window. I looked up wondering what he was talking about, then heard him say "your job's just been shot out from under you, son, you won't be going any'way'ah."*

*The date was 22 November 1963 and President John F. Kennedy had been assassinated. My Captain was right and I would remain on board* White Sage.[212]

# Epilogue

*Your descendants shall gather your fruits.*
*—Virgil*

*In an age when man has forgotten his origins and is blind even to his most essential needs for survival, water along with other resources has become the victim of his indifference.*
*—Rachel Carson*

(Allen Harbor, Harwich Port)—On the verge of June, this day in late May feels more like April; not at all summerlike. I am with Steve McKenna, the Cape and Islands regional coordinator for Massachusetts Coastal Zone Management (MA CZM), who is a Harwich-born native Cape Codder and graduate of the Massachusetts Maritime Academy with dual degrees in marine transportation and marine safety/environmental protection. Also with us is Heather Rockwell, program director for the Nantucket Soundkeeper Program and a specialist in marine education and science with a bachelor of science degree in biological oceanography from the Florida Institute of Technology. Heather is also a fellow native Cape Codder.

We're on Steve's boat, a twenty-seven-footer docked in Allen Harbor in Harwich, and we motor south toward the open Sound. Seeing the Sound up close, feeling the water, breathing in the salt air, watching the birds overhead—it's the only way to go and frankly a must-do activity for the author of a book about Nantucket Sound. We're heading due east toward Monomoy, the extreme eastern edge of the Sound, and we're about a mile off the coast where the average depth of the Sound in this area is twenty-four feet; today the water temperature is a cool sixty-four degrees at the surface. We're still at a point in the season where someone couldn't survive long periods in the waters of the open Sound.

Heather Rockwell is program officer for Nantucket Soundkeeper and Steve McKenna is the Cape and Islands regional coordinator, Massachusetts Coastal Zone Management. *Photo by Theresa M. Barbo.*

"We have so many small embayments, rivers, estuaries, inlets and coves," explains McKenna, scanning the water sheet ahead as we leave Allen Harbor in our wake. "When you think of Cape Cod Bay," he continues, "you can count on almost one hand the estuaries and the harbor areas which are off the bay. Unlike Nantucket Sound...look at the coast of Falmouth, and the different water bodies off here." As Steve talks, Heather nods in silent agreement.

Steve rattles off the ponds on the south side of Falmouth, far to our west, following a mental map heading east across the northern boundary of the Sound: "Waquoit Bay, Popponesset Bay, Barnstable's Three Bays, Lewis Bay, Parker's River, Bass River, Swan River in Dennis, Herring River in Harwich, of which there are three harbors. Onto the Stage Harbor complex in West Chatham..." Clearly, from an ecological angle, Nantucket Sound is as compelling as it is complicated.

"From a boater's point of view," insists Steve as we speed along at about ten knots, "all those estuaries and harbors and rivers create areas to explore, so you can spend a whole season exploring different places within Nantucket Sound." We're out only a few minutes before tree poles are spotted in the distance. Yes, tree poles! Inside Nantucket Sound are fishing weirs with poles to hold nets in place, a system that Native Americans used for generations before the English settled in America. We approach the circular structures—a tangle of nets and poles; there's little sign to denote which century we're in.

Our focus shifts suddenly from maritime heritage to the present, to preserve a maritime heritage for tomorrow. As pristine and beautiful as Nantucket Sound appears, it's a challenged ecosystem.

"I believe the major threats to Nantucket Sound are increased nutrient inputs, especially nitrogen, that are contributing to a degradation of water quality and, consequently, habitat degradation," clarifies Rockwell. "These nutrients are entering the coastal waters of the Sound from a variety of sources, including septic systems, boat discharges, fertilizers and storm water runoff, resulting in loss of eelgrass beds, increases in macro algae impacting benthic communities and increases in algae blooms."

The Nantucket Soundkeeper Program, after three years up and running, is analyzing data from its first two water sampling seasons. Part of Rockwell's role as program director is to oversee water quality testing. She provides this information:

> *The Nantucket Sound Water Quality Collaborative is the first comprehensive monitoring effort undertaken for Nantucket Sound. Analyses of the first two years (2006 and 2007) of water sampling data collected by the collaborative, under the technical oversight of SMAST* [School of Marine Science and Technology of UMASS-Dartmouth], *indicate that Nantucket Sound supports relatively high nitrogen-related water quality, with the highest levels of total nitrogen being observed along the south side of Cape Cod, especially in the near-shore region from Yarmouth to Chatham.*

We are nearing Stage Harbor at Chatham's extreme western waterfront. It's a small but inclusive port: a workingman's pier, filled with fishing vessels and boats dedicated to maintaining fishing weirs. Close by, however, is some of the costliest real estate in tony Chatham, tasteful but certainly large McMansions atop bluffs overlooking the water. Residential construction along historic Nantucket Sound surely increases land values but taxes the health of the ecosystem and compromises extended historical preservation.

Indeed, overdevelopment in all communities surrounding Nantucket Sound has been a concern to resource managers and decision makers for decades. Massachusetts senator Edward Kennedy's Nantucket Sound Islands Trust bill would have protected as "lands forever wild" sections within Nantucket Sound.[213] On April 11, 1972, Senator Kennedy introduced a bill to enhance preservation: "The islands covered by the legislation I am introducing include: Monomoy Island, Nantucket Island, Smith's or Esther Island, Tuckernuck Island, Muskeget Island, Martha's Vineyard Island, Noman's Land Island, and the Elizabeth Islands."[214] A total of 110,000 acres of land would have been entrusted had the bill passed. Thirty-seven years later, few could argue that the trust was an unsound idea.

Rockwell explains,

> *One of the challenges we're seeing, but not unique to the Sound, but as a shallow body of water, the problem of nitrogen loading around all the development around the rivers, estuaries and ponds, what happens…that nitrogen-rich water gets exported out into the Sound, and because the Sound has shallow warm waters during the summertime, a lot of the effects you see in the estuaries, such as algae blooms, we're seeing effects out in the Sound.*

Complicating this kettle of soup is what Heather calls the split in state and federal jurisdiction in Nantucket Sound. "The challenges facing the Sound should be addressed and regulated as a comprehensive ecosystem, not one with a 'donut hole' that impairs proper preservation and conservation of the Sound's numerous resources," she clarifies.

Finally resolved is a private company's proposal for an industrial-grade wind farm in the public trust resource that is Nantucket Sound; the wind farm is a go. The level of civic debate and discourse that this issue has raised has not been equaled on Cape Cod and the Islands since the proposed Cape Cod National Seashore and, before that, Prohibition.

Additionally, the draft of the first-ever ocean management plan mandated under the state's Oceans Act of 2008, the cutting-edge and innovative work of Cape & Islands State Senator Robert O'Leary, was publicly launched by the commonwealth's Executive Office of Energy and Environmental Affairs in summer 2009.

> *We should preserve every scrap of biodiversity as priceless while we learn to use it and come to understand what it means to humanity.*
> —*E.O. Wilson*

# APPENDICES

## A Walk Along Nantucket Sound's Coastline

By Gil Newton
Sandwich High School and Cape Cod Community College
Author of *Seaweeds of Cape Cod*

One of the reasons that southern Cape Cod is so fascinating to study is because of its rich coastal biological diversity. Nantucket Sound covers an area around twenty-five miles wide and thirty miles long. The shorelines of the Cape and Islands are characterized by a variety of marine habitats, including salt marshes, barrier beaches and estuaries. These systems are both ecologically and economically important. Their special status is the result of the warm southern Gulf Stream mixing with the colder northern Labrador current.

The waters and coastal habitats of Nantucket Sound harbor many protected and endangered animals, including several species of sea turtles, gray seals and piping plovers. But these are just the most well-known marine animals. There are many more species in this region, all of which contribute to the area's remarkable diversity.

Let's consider some of the significant habitats along these shores. Salt marshes are considered the most productive coastal systems, supporting large numbers of commercial shellfish and finfish populations. Marshes are composed of several conspicuous grass species that provide food and shelter to dozens of different animals. *Spartina alterniflora*, or cordgrass, is a tall, perennial species that buffers the edge of a marsh and provides food by direct grazing, or decomposed plant material in the form of detritus. Large mats of cordgrass are transported out to sea at high tide to be consumed by small animals in the water column.

The bulk of the marsh is composed of *Spartina patens*, or salt marsh hay. This plant grows farther from the water's edge and also contributes to the productivity of the marsh. Small marsh snails crawl to the tops of the marsh hay blades during high tide. Large populations of fiddler crabs scurry around at low tide. These crustaceans are important ecologically as a food source for birds that aerate the peat with their burrows and fertilize the sediments with their wastes.

Salt marshes, and the bays that sometimes surround them, are also homes to commercially important species such as quahogs, oysters and scallops. Blue crabs, spider crabs and mud snails can be seen feeding in the creeks. Small schools of mummichogs move into the creeks with the high tide. Occasionally, a horseshoe crab can be seen stranded in one of the numerous pools, or pans.

Sometimes salt marshes are part of a larger system known as a barrier beach. A long sand dune community may separate the open sandy beach from an estuary and salt marsh behind it. The estuary is influenced by the ocean and a source of fresh water, either a stream, river or groundwater. There are over two hundred barrier beaches in Massachusetts, but one of my favorites is a small system in Osterville called Dowses Beach. This is a popular recreational beach in the summer, and is characterized by several "microhabitats" linked and interacting together. The sandy beach is often covered with thousands of slipper snail shells, often tangled with the invasive green alga *Codium*. At low tide, small sanderlings and herring gulls can be seen foraging in the intertidal zone for mole crabs and burrowing worms. Overall, this zone is a relatively hostile environment for living things because of the constant wave action and rapid changes in temperature, salinity and oxygen concentration.

The sand dune community has an entirely different assemblage of plants and animals. Beach grass is abundant and helps hold the dune in place with its strong, adventitious roots. However, there are other plant species that make up the plant community, including dusty miller, beach pea, wormwood and seaside goldenrod. The introduced salt spray rose (*Rosa rugosa*) provides colorful pink and white flowers to the dunes during the summer.

Animal life here represents a transition zone between the marine and terrestrial environments. The protected piping plovers will nest in the open areas, nearly indistinguishable from the sand. Diamondback terrapins make the Cape their northernmost distribution point and can be found laying their eggs in the dunes. Of course, this is also the habitat for the notorious deer tick. The deer tick can inject the bacterium that causes Lyme disease if it bites you.

There are a number of important bays and estuaries that exist along the southern Cape shore, including East Bay in Osterville and Waquoit Bay in Falmouth. These ecosystems are major nurseries for fish populations and resting places for migratory birds. Most of these bodies of water are sheltered and are therefore attractive to species seeking food, habitat and protection from predators.

Unfortunately, many of these coastal habitats are exhibiting environmental stress from the pressures of increased human populations. One major coastal problem is nitrogen loading, which acts as a fertilizer, resulting in harmful algae blooms. The nitrogen is coming from septic systems, road runoff, lawn fertilizers and the atmosphere, due to the burning of fossil fuels. When the algae die and decompose, the bacteria responsible for decomposition consume oxygen dissolved in the water. Large mats of algae such as *Codium* can block sunlight to subtidal eelgrass beds.

Even recreational uses of sandy beaches can have an adverse effect on these fragile systems if not properly managed. Marine debris can choke and entangle pelagic birds and marine mammals. Nesting sites of endangered bird species such as piping plovers and least terns can be disrupted if not correctly identified and marked. And, as described earlier, excess nitrogen can seriously damage bays and estuaries.

These critical coastal systems of Nantucket Sound can continue to be enjoyed and sustained for future generations if we remain vigilant in our efforts to understand and protect them. Continued scientific research is the key to maintaining and managing these resources. Fortunately, one of the communities in this region is Woods Hole, with its eminent research facilities such as the Marine Biological Laboratory and the Woods Hole Oceanographic Institution. These organizations, along with the many local conservation groups, are perfectly situated to provide data and guidance for this unique and vital region.

## Waquoit Bay: Mashpee's Area of Critical Environmental Concern (ACEC)

By Lisa Berry-Engler
ACEC Coastal Coordinator
Massachusetts Department of Conservation and Recreation

*Areas of Critical Environmental Concern (ACECs) are places in Massachusetts that contain natural and cultural resources of regional, state or national importance. The*

Waquoit Bay is recognized as an Area of Critical Environmental Concern by MA CZM. *Courtesy of Massachusetts Coastal Zone Management.*

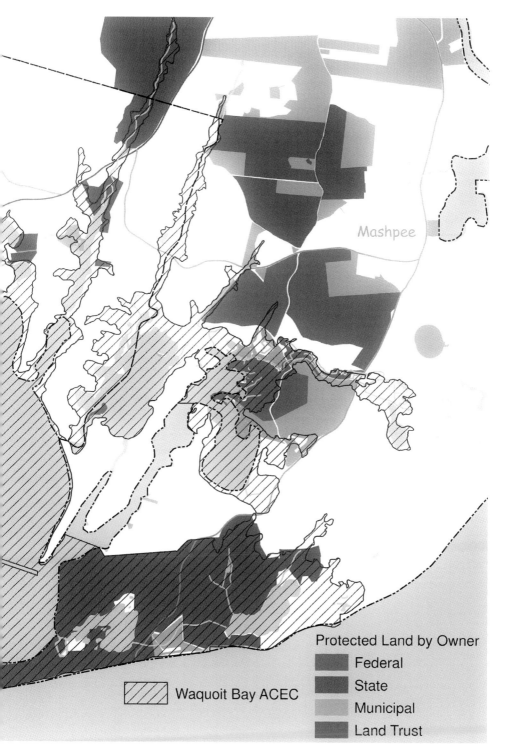

Mashpee

Protected Land by Owner

■ Federal
■ State
■ Municipal
■ Land Trust

▨ Waquoit Bay ACEC

*thirty state-designated ACECs range in size from 160 to 37,450 acres. The purpose of the ACEC Program is to preserve, restore and enhance these exceptional resources. For more information, please visit the ACEC website at* http://www.mass.gov/dcr/stewardship/acec.

ACECs are places in Massachusetts that receive special recognition because of the quality, uniqueness and significance of their natural and cultural resources. These areas are identified and nominated at the community level and are reviewed and designated by the state's secretary of energy and environmental affairs. The purpose of the ACEC Program is to preserve, restore and enhance critical environmental and cultural resources and natural resource areas of the commonwealth. The goals of the ACEC Program are to identify and designate these important ecological areas, increase the level of protection for ACECs and facilitate and support the stewardship of ACECs. ACEC designation increases public awareness and education about the exceptional natural and cultural resources within ACECs and creates a framework for local and regional protection, management and stewardship.

Established in 1975 by legislation that created the Massachusetts Executive Office of Environmental Affairs, the ACEC Program has worked to protect the state's critical resources for more than thirty years. Currently, the ACEC Program oversees the preservation, restoration and enhancement of a wealth of diverse cultural and natural resources in thirty coastal and inland ACECs. Fourteen of these ACECs are considered coastal, in that they lie within the coastal zone (the area between three miles offshore and one hundred feet beyond the first major land transportation route encountered on shore (a road, highway, rail line, etc.) and including all of Cape Cod and the Islands). Of the fourteen coastal ACECs, nine are found in the Cape Cod/Plymouth region and one borders Nantucket Sound. The Waquoit Bay ACEC is located in the towns of Falmouth and Mashpee and was designated in 1979. "Waquoit" is the name used by the Mashpee tribe, which settled in this region.

The Waquoit Bay ACEC encompasses 2,575 acres of estuarine and adjacent upland habitat. The ACEC includes most of the Waquoit Bay National Estuarine Research Reserve and portions of the surrounding Mashpee National Wildlife Refuge (MNWR). The entire bay is designated by the state as an Ocean Sanctuary. Important habitats within the boundary include estuarine waters, freshwater wetlands and ponds, shrub and wooded swamps, streams, salt marsh, tidal flats, coastal dunes and beaches. The diverse and relatively unaltered habitats provide feeding, spawning and nursery grounds for numerous shellfish, finfish, amphibians, reptiles, birds and mammals. Waquoit Bay provides flood control, storm damage prevention, water quality protection, wildlife habitat for upland and estuarine species and recreational opportunities for the surrounding communities. The Waquoit Bay ACEC also contains many significant archaeological sites.

Stewardship, or active management and oversight, plays a key role in the protection of ACEC resources after an area is designated. ACEC stewards can be local, state or federal organizations, individuals or a collaborative partnership among all or some of these groups. The ACEC Program relies on volunteer stewards to guide stewardship activities, help raise awareness about the resources of the ACEC, set management priorities and help provide oversight and public comment when inappropriate development, water quality degradation or misuse of resources could threaten the critical resources of the ACEC.

The Waquoit Bay ACEC benefits from the cooperative stewardship of many partners with interests in the management and protection of the bay. The Waquoit Bay area is part of the National Estuarine Research Reserve System (NERRS), a federal-state partnership between the U.S. Department of Commerce, National Atmospheric and Oceanic Administration (NOAA) and the Massachusetts Department of Conservation and Recreation (DCR). As a reserve in the NERRS, Waquoit Bay serves as a natural laboratory for field research and monitoring while protecting the existing ecological, economic, recreational and aesthetic values of the ecosystem. The Waquoit Bay NERR collects and disseminates this research to local citizens and decision makers. The boundaries of the NERR are almost identical to those of the Waquoit Bay ACEC.

Much land within and adjacent to the Waquoit Bay ACEC is protected by the DCR, other state agencies, local land trusts and the Towns of Falmouth and Mashpee. These landowners preserve and protect land within the Waquoit Bay watershed, which improves water quality, provides habitat and allows for recreational activities within a highly developed region. Other stewardship partners of the Waquoit Bay ACEC include the Citizens for the Protection of Waquoit Bay, the official friends group of the Waquoit Bay NERR and the Mashpee NWR Partners group. The Citizens for the Protection of Waquoit Bay, active since the early 1980s, provides education about the environment and the connection between land use and estuarine ecosystem health. The Mashpee NWR Partners group coordinates the many protection and management activities within Waquoit Bay. Members include representatives from many of the stewardship groups and other state and federal agencies, nonprofits and local residents.

# Nantucket Sound and the
# Cape Cod National Seashore

By William Burke
Historian and Cultural Resources Program Manager
Cape Cod National Seashore

Blanketing the southeastern flank of the lands of Cape Cod National Seashore, Nantucket Sound appears to be an uninterested neighbor with no shared interests or resources with the great Outer Beach. Yet the Sound's geographical position and historical legacy complement the National Seashore's geology, ecosystems and human history. The early visionaries working on a proposal for a national seashore recognized the Sound's calmer, warmer waters, kid-friendly surf and proximity to mid-Cape villages and included Harding's Beach and Stage and Morris Islands in the first draft boundary. Although these locations were removed in later versions of the proposed park, today's National Seashore slivers southward beyond Chatham along the ever-shifting strand known as South Beach. This beach, along with the immense Monomoy National Wildlife Refuge, frames the easternmost reaches of the Sound. Although the connection is thin, the comparisons of Sound to Seashore hold a few notable shared threads.

First, there is the common geologic ancestry. Both the Sound and the Seashore were born from the last ice age. Both are composed of glacial outwash and now shaped by rising sea level and coastal erosion. The National Seashore's Outer Beach is exposed to the full wave attack of the open Atlantic, whereas the Sound's shallow basin dampens wave energy, warms local waters and sustains life. Flora and fauna are another common thread, although critters like the blue crab respond to a temperature boundary and are reluctant to move north of the warmer Sound waters. Migrating shorebirds certainly utilize the divergent habitats of both places, as does beach grass and salt spray rose. The earliest native people freely roamed both locations, as did early European explorers. Exceptions were Champlain, whose extreme difficulties in passing from Outer Beach to the Sound south of Chatham may have thwarted French colonization efforts beyond Canada, and the 1620 Pilgrims, whose attempt to reach the mouth of the Hudson Valley was prevented by the same area of hazardous shoals; they diverted their sights north to Plymouth. Later mariners viewed the outer arm of the Cape as a gauntlet to be run, while the Sound offered refuge and safe harbor. Thirteen lifesaving stations dotted the Outer Beach by 1900.

Ultimately, the physical palette of Nantucket Sound shaped its human story, etching upon it a sense of place. Its more sheltered exposure from storms, wind, waves and erosion and its pleasant sandy beaches and access to good roads and railroad invited early and intense resort development along its shores and islands by the early twentieth century. At the same time, the wilder lands of the future National Seashore, buffeted by nor'easters, shipwrecks and cold surf, went largely unnoticed until post World War II. By August 7, 1961, when President John F. Kennedy signed the legislation preserving forty-four thousand acres of the Cape Cod National Seashore, most of the lands adjacent to the Sound were largely developed. President Kennedy declared, "I...hope that this will be one of a whole series of great seashore parks which will be for the inspiration and enjoyment of people all over the United States." Since then, other national seashores indeed have been created, but Cape Cod's has become one of the nation's most popular parks, with more than five million visitors each year. No doubt, Kennedy's exposure to the joys of Nantucket Sound from his Hyannisport compound inspired him to persevere in the long effort to protect the contrasting landscape of Cape Cod National Seashore.

# NOTES

## Chapter One

1. Victor Mastone, interview with the author, May 2009.
2. Ibid.
3. Ibid.
4. Barry Homer, interview with the author, May 2009.
5. Terry Clen, interview with the author, April 2009.
6. Ibid.
7. Douglas-Lithgow, *Nantucket: A History*, 5.
8. Ibid.
9. Ibid.
10. Ibid., 6.
11. Ibid., 18.
12. Ibid., 6.
13. Ibid., 7–11.
14. Ibid., 18.
15. Provincetown Center for Coastal Studies, "Toward an Ocean Vision," 9.
16. Provincetown Center for Coastal Studies, "Review of State," 3.
17. Provincetown Center for Coastal Studies, "Toward an Ocean Vision," 2.
18. Susan Nickerson, interview with the author, May 2009.
19. Ibid.
20. Provincetown Center for Coastal Studies, "Toward an Ocean Vision," 27.
21. Heather Rockwell, interview with the author, May 2009.
22. Ibid.
23. Ibid.
24. Lee F. Gruzen, interview with the author, June 2009.
25. Ibid.

26. Nicole Miller, "Weathering the Hurricane of 1944," *Yarmouth Register*, Wednesday, October 26, 2005, 1.
27. Susan Nickerson, interview with the author, May 2009.
28. Bowditch, *New American Practical Navigator*, 7.

# Chapter Two

29. Banks, *History of Martha's Vineyard*, 47.
30. Linda Coombs, interview with the author, June 2009.
31. Banks, *History of Martha's Vineyard*, 55.
32. Coombs interview.
33. Huntington, "Character and Life Style of the Indians," 194.
34. Coombs interview.
35. Ibid.
36. Banks, *History of Martha's Vineyard*, 46.
37. Ibid., 52.
38. Ibid., 39.
39. Ibid.
40. Ibid.
41. Scoville, *Indian Legends of Martha's Vineyard*, 3.
42. Banks, *History of Martha's Vineyard*, 59.
43. Travers, *Wampanoag Indian Federation*, 58.
44. Coombs interview.
45. Banks, *History of Martha's Vineyard*, 65.
46. Travers, *Wampanoag Indian Federation*, 58.
47. Gookin, *Capawack*, 9.
48. Several paragraphs about Thomas Mayhew Jr. and his mission work were scanned from *Martha's Vineyard* by Henry Franklin Norton and can be found at http://history.vineyard.net/hfnorton/history.htm.
49. Ibid., 5.
50. Ibid., 6.
51. Mayhew, *Pious Indian Women*, vi.
52. Coombs interview.
53. Brenizer, *Nantucket Indians*, 33.
54. Ibid., 38.
55. Ibid.
56. Elizabeth A. Little, Probate Records of Nantucket Indians. Nantucket Historical Association, 1980.
57. Philbrick, *Abram's Eyes*, 202.

58. Ibid., 200.
59. Ibid., 202.
60. Ibid., 203.
61. Douglas-Lithgow, *Nantucket: A History*, 270.
62. Philbrick, *Abram's Eyes*, 236.

## Chapter Three

63. Originally published in *Historic Nantucket* 49, no. 1 (Winter 2000): 12–38, made available at http://www.nha.org/history/hn/HN-winter2000-timeline.htm, 1.
64. Ibid.
65. Ibid.
66. Ibid.
67. Vickers, "First Whalemen of Nantucket," 561.
68. Bliss, *Quaint Nantucket*, 6.
69. Ibid.
70. Originally published in *Historic Nantucket* 49, no. 1 (Winter 2000): 12–38, made available at www.nha.org/history/hn/HN-winter2000-timeline.htm, 1.
71. Bliss, *Quaint Nantucket*, 7.
72. Ibid., 12.
73. Byrne, *Nantucket Jetties*. Originally published in *Historic Nantucket* 48, no. 4 (Fall 1999): 14–16. Made available at www.nha.org/history/hn/HN-fall99-jetties.htm, 1.
74. Ibid., 14–15.
75. Ibid., 16.
76. Originally published in *Historic Nantucket* 49, no. 1 (Winter 2000): 12–38, made available at www.nha.org/history/hn/HN-winter2000-timeline.htm, 20.
77. Crevecoeur, *Letters from an American Farmer*, Letter IV, 48. Information can be found at http://xroads.virginia.edu/~HYPER/CREV/letter04.html.
78. Norton, *Martha's Vineyard*, 4.
79. Deyo, *History of Barnstable County*, 708.
80. Ibid., 633.
81. GenealogyResearchCenter.org, Land Records for Genealogy & Family Tree Research, Section 18, 1.
82. Deyo, *History of Barnstable County*, 634.

83. Swift, "Swift Family Whaling," 20.

84. Ibid., 23.

85. Railton, *History of Martha's Vineyard*, 187.

86. Smith, *Woods Hole Reflections*, 54.

87. Ibid., 55.

88. Ibid.

89. Allen, *Brief History of Woods Hole*.

90. Pacific Guano Company, reprinted from *Falmouth Enterprise*, May 16, 1961, 55.

91. Allen, *Brief History of Woods Hole*.

92. Ibid., 4.

93. Ibid.

94. Ibid., 5.

95. Ibid.

96. Ibid., 6.

97. Deyo, *History of Barnstable County*, 635.

98. Ibid., 358.

99. Ibid., 369.

100. Ibid.

101. Ibid.

102. Ibid., 370.

103. Grayson, *Cape Cod Catboats*, 16.

104. Chesbro, *Osterville*, 1.

105. Ibid.

106. Ibid.

107. Ibid., 10.

108. Ibid.

109. Honorable Charles S. Swift and Deyo, *History of Barnstable County*, 454. Simeon L. Deyo was editor of the seminal tome *The History of Barnstable County, Massachusetts*. While skimming citations in this section you may also see the work of the Honorable Charles S. Swift listed as co-author. This is not an error; Swift contributed to sections of the book and where his byline is mentioned within various chapters, I have included his name alongside Deyo's.

110. Ibid., 455.

111. Ibid.

112. Ibid., 460.

113. Phyllis Horton, interview with the author, May 2009.

114. Ibid.

115. Ibid.

116. Horton, "An Assortment of Rumrunners."
117. Chesbro, *Osterville*, 45.
118. Deyo, *History of Barnstable County*, 533.
119. Ibid., 535.
120. Paine, *History of Harwich*, 29.
121. Ibid.
122. Ibid., 30.
123. Freeman, *History of Cape Cod*, 492.
124. Ibid., 493.
125. Ibid., 495.
126. Ibid., 492.
127. Ibid.
128. Ibid., 579.
129. Ibid.
130. Deyo, *History of Barnstable County, Massachusetts*, 581.
131. Ibid.
132. Ibid., 595.
133. Lawrence, *Journal of Occurrences*, 22.
134. Swift and Deyo, *History of Barnstable County, Massachusetts*, 466.
135. Paine, *History of Harwich*, 319.
136. McCullough, *1776*, 73.

# Chapter Four

137. Swift and Deyo, *History of Barnstable County*, 467.
138. Deyo, *History of Barnstable County*, 524.
139. Ibid., 582.
140. Burton N. Derick, interview with the author, May 2009.
141. Information for the section entitled "Bustling Wharves in Harwich" was derived from *Harwich Vessels*, which was researched and prepared by the Sidney Brooks Scholars at Brooks Academy Museum in Harwich, Cape Cod, Massachusetts, in 1998. I am indebted to Dr. John Roche for his assistance.
142. Chesbro, *Osterville*, 13.
143. Douglas-Lithgow, *Nantucket: A History*, 270.
144. Ibid.
145. All information about Nathaniel Wixon of Dennis was courtesy of his grandson, historian Burton N. Derick.
146. Little, "Drift Whales At Nantucket."

147. Ibid.
148. Vickers, *First Whalemen of Nantucket*, 560.
149. Originally published in *Historic Nantucket* 49, no. 1 (Winter 2000): 12–38, made available at www.nha.org/history/hn/HN-winter2000-timeline. htm, 2.
150. Ibid.
151. Ibid.
152. Paine, *History of Harwich*, 303.
153. Ibid., 306.
154. Morrison, *Maritime History of Massachusetts*, 20.
155. *Falmouth Enterprise*, July 1925.
156. Ibid.
157. Logue, "Whaling Industry," 427.
158. Ibid.
159. Ibid., 433.
160. Ibid.
161. Ibid., 436.
162. Crevecoeur, *Letters from an American Farmer*, 48. Information can be found at http://xroads.virginia.edu/~HYPER/CREV/letter04.html.
163. Logue, "Whaling Industry," 434.
164. Clark, "American Whale-Fishery," 321.
165. Ibid.
166. Ibid.
167. Ibid.
168. Ibid.

## Chapter Five

169. Sechrest, "Public Goods and Private Solutions," 4.
170. Ibid.
171. Correspondence between Captain Henry Manter (1816–1878) and his wife, Mary, is located at the Martha's Vineyard Museum and is liberally quoted in this chapter. The Manters lived in Holmes Hole, later Vineyard Haven. Captain Henry Manter was the subject of an extensive biography composed by Arthur R. Railton in the February 2001 edition of the *Intelligencer* 42, no. 3.
172. Archives of the Dennis Historical Society, with the assistance of curator Phyllis Horton.
173. Morris, *Captain from Cape Cod*, 97.

174. Ibid.

175. Ibid.

176. Stackpole, *Sea-Hunters*, 222.

177. Ibid.

178. Ibid., 223.

179. Ibid.

180. Originally published in *Historic Nantucket* 49, no. 1 (Winter 2000): 12–38, made available at www.nha.org/history/hn/HN-winter2000-timeline. htm, 20.

181. Stackpole, *Sea-Hunters*, 225.

182. Ibid.

183. Kittredge, *Shipmasters of Cape Cod*, 238.

184. For key information on the colorful Captain Zeb Tilton (1866–1952) of Martha's Vineyard, I solely relied upon the work of Polly Burroughs, who composed *Zeb*.

185. Turner, *Story of the Island Steamers*, 2.

186. Ibid., 8.

187. Ibid., 9.

188. James P. Warbasse, "From Sail to Steam to Diesel," 17.

189. Ibid., 16.

190. Ibid.

191. Turner, *Story of the Island Steamers*, 15.

192. Ibid.

193. Ibid.

194. Burroughs, *Zeb*, 58.

# Chapter Six

195. Letter from William Garfield of West Dennis to President James A. Garfield. These and other letters are from the personal papers of President James A. Garfield in the Library of Congress [177 reel], though they were provided to me by a Garfield descendant, Lee F. Gruzen. "Since it appears that most every Garfield in America wrote the president to ask for a favor or supply him with genealogical information, something Garfield truly enjoyed, this source is invaluable for researchers," shared Gruzen.

196. My chief source for lighthouses was Donald Davidson's book, *America's Landfall*. I recall hearing Davidson lecture on the subject, years ago, and I feel that there's no better local authority. Since there would have been numerous citations from this sole source, I did not include the string of Ibids here.

197. For the lightship section, I relied on Frederick L. Thompson's *Lightships of Cape Cod*. Rather than clutter this section with numerous citations, and since his was the chief source, I mention the book here. The two places where I drew information from the written work of Harwich harbormaster Tom Leach in his article "The Lightships of Nantucket Sound" are attributed within the central text.

198. I am especially in debt to Maurice Gibbs of Nantucket, who provided the chronology, guidance, advice and quotes on the section on lifesavers, unless otherwise cited. His assistance was invaluable.

199. Kennedy, "Impeachment of Andrew Johnson."

200. Ibid., 1.

201. Ibid.

202. Means, "Heavy Sea Running."

203. Ibid., 3.

204. Ibid.

205. *Boston Globe*, "Five Men Saved, Daring Rescue from a Sinking Ship," n.d.

206. Ibid.

207. *Harwich Independent*, July 11, 1899.

208. Ibid.

209. Ibid.

210. D.C. Baldinelli, "U.S. Coast Guard," 2.

211. After his command tour in Woods Hole, Captain W. Russell Webster was chief of rescue operations for Coast Guard District One in Boston until his retirement in 2003. He is currently the federal preparedness coordinator for the Federal Emergency Management Agency's New England office in Boston and is a maritime historian specializing in Cape Cod Coast Guard cases.

212. Before his sudden death of a heart attack in January 2009, Mr. Webber shared with me a number of essays from his days in the Coast Guard, in which he served from 1946 until 1966. This essay is part of that collection, which remains, to date, unpublished.

# Epilogue

213. John Blumenthal, "Nantucket Would Rather Protect Itself," *Christian Science Monitor*, Wednesday, May 24, 1972, 4.

214. Congressional Record-Senate, April 11, 1972.

# BIBLIOGRAPHY

Albion, Robert G., William A. Baker and Benjamin W. Labaree. *New England and the Sea*. Mystic, CT: Marine Historical Association, Inc., 1972.

Allen, Norman T. *A Brief History of Woods Hole*. Paper delivered before Falmouth Historical Association, 1966.

Baker, Florence W. *Yesterday's Tide*. South Yarmouth, MA: self-published, 1941.

Baldinelli, D.C., LCDR. "The U.S. Coast Guard's Assignment to the Department of Homeland Security: Entering Unchartered Waters or Just a Course Correction?" Essay, December 9, 2002.

Bangs, Jeremy Dupertuis. *Indian Deeds: Land Transactions in Plymouth Colony, 1620–1691*. Boston: New England Historic Genealogical Society, 2002.

Banks, Charles Edward, MD. *The History of Martha's Vineyard, Dukes County, Massachusetts, Volumes I, II & III*. Edgartown, MA: Dukes County Historical Society, 1966.

*Barnstable Patriot*

Beatley, Timothy, David J. Brower and Anna K. Schwab. *An Introduction to Coastal Zone Management, Second Edition*. Washington, D.C.: Island Press, 2002.

Bliss, William Root. *Quaint Nantucket.* Cambridge, MA: Houghton, Mifflin & Company, 1896.

*Boston Globe*

Bowditch, Nathaniel. *The New American Practical Navigator.* New York: E.& G.W. Blunt Proprietors, 1865.

Brenizer, Meredith Marshall. *The Nantucket Indians—Legends and Accounts before 1659.* Nantucket, MA: Meredith Marshall Brenizer, 1976.

Bunting, W.H., comp. and annotator. *Portrait of a Port Boston, 1852–1914.* Cambridge, MA: Belknap Press of Harvard University Press, 1971.

Burroughs, Polly. *Zeb: Celebrated Schooner Captain of Martha's Vineyard.* Guilford, CT: Globe Pequot Press, 2005.

Byrne, Matt. *Nantucket Jetties.* Originally published in *Historic Nantucket* 48, no. 4 (Fall 1999): 14–16. Made available at www.nha.org/history/hn/HN-fall99-jetties.htm.

*Cape Cod Times*

Carr, Elliott. *Walking the Shores of Cape Cod.* Yarmouth Port, MA: On Cape Publications, 1997.

Carson, Rachel L. *Silent Spring.* New York: Houghton Mifflin Company, 1962.

Chapelle, Howard I. *The History of American Sailing Ships.* New York: W.W. Norton & Company, Inc., 1935.

Chesbro, Paul L. *Osterville, Volume I.* Taunton, MA: William S. Sullwold Publishing, Inc., 1988.

———.*Osterville, Volume II.* Taunton, MA: William S. Sullwold Publishing, Inc., 1989.

*Christian Science Monitor*

Clark, A. Howard. "The American Whale-Fishery, 1877–1886." *Science* 9 (April 1, 1887).

Clifford, Mary Louise, and Candace Clifford. *Women Who Kept the Lights: An Illustrated History of Female Lighthouse Keepers.* Alexandria, VA: Cypress Communications, 1993.

Congressional Record

Crevecoeur, J. Hector St. John. *Letters from an American Farmer.* Reprinted New York: Fox, Duffield, 1904.

Dalton, J.W. *The Lifesavers of Cape Cod.* 1902. Reprinted Orleans, MA: Parnassus Imprints, 1991.

D'Amico, Zabelle. *The Breeds and the Caretakers of their Englewood Legacy.* Yarmouth Port, MA: Historical Society of Old Yarmouth, 1998.

Davidson, Daniel. Personal interview with the author, May 2009.

Davidson, Donald W. *America's Landfall: Historic Lighthouses of Cape Cod, Nantucket & Martha's Vineyard.* Fourth Edition. Cape Cod, MA: Peninsula Press, 1993.

Dayton, Fred Erving. *Steamboat Days.* New York: Frederick A. Stokes, Co., 1925.

*Dennis Historical Society Newsletter* 17, no. 10 (October 1994).

Derick, Burton N. Personal interview with the author, May 2009.

Deyo, Simeon L. *The History of Barnstable County, Massachusetts.* New York: H.W. Blake & Co., 1890.

Dodge, Ernest S., ed. *Thirty Years of the American Neptune.* Cambridge, MA: Harvard University Press, 1972.

Douglas-Lithgow, R.A., MD, LLD. *Nantucket: A History.* New York and London: G.P. Putnam's Sons, 1914.

Dow, George Francis. *Every Day Life in the Massachusetts Bay Colony*. Mineola, NY: Dover Publications, 1988.

*Dukes County Intelligencer*. "Those Elegant Steamers of Yesterday." May 1983, 147.

Earle, Sylvia A. *Sea Change: A Message of the Oceans*. New York: Ballantine Books, 1995.

Engle, Eloise, and Arnold S. Lott. *America's Maritime Heritage*. Annapolis, MD: United States Naval Institute, 1975.

Evans, Sylvanus Crowell. Notebook. Transcribed by Burton N. Derick, July 1998.

Freeman, Frederick. *A History of Cape Cod: The Annals of Barnstable County and of Its Several Towns*. Boston: reprinted for the author, 1858.

Gardner, Arthur H., comp. *Wrecks Around Nantucket*. New Bedford, MA: Reynolds Printing, Inc., 1915.

Gookin, Warner Foote. *Capawack, alias Martha's Vineyard*. Edgartown, MA: Dukes County Historical Society, 1947.

Grayson, Stan. *Cape Cod Catboats*. Marblehead, MA: Devereux Books, 2002.

Guthorn, Peter J. "America's Last Independent Hydrographer." *Imago Mundi: The International Journal for the History of Cartography* 43, no. 1 (1991): 72–80.

*Harwich Independent*

Hawke, David Freeman. *Everyday Life in Early America*. New York: Harper & Rowe Publishers, 1988.

Heyrman, Christine Leigh. *Commerce and Culture: The Maritime Communities of Colonial Massachusetts, 1690–1750*. New York: W.W. Norton & Company, Inc., 1984.

Homer, Barry. Personal interview with the author, April 2009.

Horton, Phyllis. "An Assortment of Rumrunners." *Dennis Historical Society Newsletter* 17, no. 10 (October 1994).

———. Personal interview with the author, May 2009.

Huntington, Gale. "The Character and Life Style of the Indians." *Nantucket Intelligencer*, August 1995.

Johnston, James C., Jr. *The Yankee Fleet, Maritime New England in the Age of Sail.* Charleston, SC: The History Press, 2007.

*Journal of Martha's Vineyard and the Elizabeth Islands.*

Kennedy, Robert C. "The Impeachment of Andrew Johnson." *HarpWeek*, 1998–2005.

Kittredge, Henry C. *Cape Cod: Its People and Their History*. Boston: Houghton Mifflin Company, 1968.

———. *Mooncussers of Cape Cod*. Boston and New York: Houghton Mifflin Company, 1937.

———. *Shipmasters of Cape Cod*. Reprinted Hyannis, MA: Parnassus Imprints, 1988.

Labaree, Benjamin W., William M. Fowler Jr., John B. Hattendorf, Jeffrey J. Safford, Edward W. Sloan and Andrew W. German. *America and the Sea: A Maritime History*. Mystic, CT: Mystic Seaport Museum, Inc., 1998.

Lawrence, Frederick V., Jr. *A Journal of Occurrences along the Rebel Coast.* Westminster, MD: Heritage Books, 2008.

LifeSavingService.org

Little, Elizabeth A. "Drift Whales At Nantucket: The Kindness of Moshup." Nantucket Historical Association.

Logue, Barbara J. "The Whaling Industry and Fertility Decline." *Social Science History* 7, no. 4 (Fall 1983).

Lombard, Asa Cobb Paine, Jr. *East of Cape Cod.* New Bedford, MA: Reynolds-DeWalt Printing, Inc., 1976.

Luther, B.W., comp. *Marine Disasters of Martha's Vineyard.* Sandwich, MA: Published by Peter Closson, 1970.

Martha's Vineyard Historical Society. Record Unit 179 Captain Henry Manter Papers 1841–1913. By Karin Stanley.

Mayhew, Experience. *Narratives of the Lives of Pious Indian Women Who Lived on Martha's Vineyard More Than One Hundred Years Since.* Boston: James Loring, 1830.

McCullough, David. *1776.* New York: Simon & Schuster, 2005.

Means, Dennis R. "A Heavy Sea Running: The Formation of the U.S. Life-Saving Service, 1846–1878." 1987.

Miele, Leonard. *Voice of the Tide: The Cape Cod Heritage of Katharine Lee Bates.* New Bedford, MA: Spinner Publications, 2009.

Miller, Stauffer. *Hoisting Their Colors, Cape Cod's Civil War Navy Officers.* N.p.: Xlibris Corporation. 2008.

Morgan, Edmund S. *The Puritan Dilemma: The Story of John Winthrop.* Canada: Little, Brown & Company, 1950.

Morris, Paul C. *A Captain from Cape Cod: The Merchant Fleets of Crowell & Thurlow.* Orleans, MA: Lower Cape Publications, 2002.

———. *Maritime Nantucket: A Pictorial History of the "Little Grey Lady of the Sea."* Orleans, MA: Lower Cape Publications, 1996.

Morrison, Samuel Eliot. *Maritime History of Massachusetts, 1783–1860.* Boston: Houghton Mifflin Company, 1921.

*Nantucket Inquirer & Mirror*

Nickerson, Geraldine D. *Chatham Sea Captains in the Age of Sail.* Charleston, SC: The History Press, 2007.

Norton, Henry Franklin. *Martha's Vineyard.* N.p.: Henry Norton and Robert Emmett Pyne, Publishers, 1923.

O'Neill, J.P. *The Great New England Sea Serpent.* Camden, ME: Down East Books, 1999.

Oppel, Frank. *Tales of the New England Coast.* Secaucus, NJ: Castle and Book Sales, Inc., 1985.

Paine, Josiah. *A History of Harwich, Mass. 1620–1800.* Reprinted Salem, MA: Higginson Book Company, 1937.

Peirce, Ebenezer W. *Indian History, Biography and Genealogy.* North Abington, MA: Zerviah Gould Mitchell, 1878.

Philbrick, Nathaniel. *Abram's Eyes.* Nantucket, MA: Mill Hill Press, 1998.

Provincetown Center for Coastal Studies. "Review of State and Federal Marine Protection of the Ecological Resources of Nantucket Sound." January 2003.

———. "Toward an Ocean Vision for the Nantucket Shelf Region." Prepared by Jo Ann Muramoto and Richard Delaney, Horsley Witten Group, Inc., January 2005.

Quinn, William P. *Cape Cod Maritime Disasters.* Orleans, MA: Lower Cape Publishing, 1990.

Railton, Arthur R. "Capt. Henry Manter of Holmes Hole: A Lifetime on the World's Oceans." *Dukes County Intelligencer,* February 2001.

———. "Captain Manter's Last Whaling Voyage: Four Years in the Pacific Aboard *Virginia.*" *Dukes County Intelligencer,* August 2001, 9–37.

———. *The History of Martha's Vineyard.* Beverly, MA: Commonwealth Editions, 2006.

Rediker, Marcus. *Between the Devil and the Deep Blue Sea.* New York: Cambridge University Press, 1987.

*The Register*

Reid, Nancy Thacher. *Dennis, Cape Cod*. Dennis, MA: Dennis Historical Society, 1996.

Reynard, Elizabeth. *The Narrow Land, Folk Chronicles of Old Cape Cod*. Boston: Houghton Mifflin Company, 1962.

Rongner, George E. *Life Aboard a Coast Guard Lightship*. West Conshohocken, PA: InfinityPublishing.com, 2007.

Russell, Howard S. *Indian New England Before the Mayflower*. Hanover, NH: University Press of New England, 1980.

Schroeder, John H. *Shaping a Maritime Empire—The Commercial and Diplomatic Role of the American Navy, 1829–1861*. Westport, CT: Greenwood Press, 1985.

Schultz, Eric B., and Michael J. Tougias. *King Philip's War*. Woodstock, VT: The Countryman Press, 1999.

Schwarzman, Beth. *The Nature of Cape Cod*. 2002. University Press of New England: Hanover, New Hampshire.

Scoville, Dorothy R. *Indian Legends of Martha's Vineyard*. Gay Head, MA: Dorothy Radcliffe Scoville, 1970.

*Scribner's Monthly.* "The United States Life-Saving Service." Vol. 12, no. 3 (January 1880).

*Seafaring in Colonial Massachusetts*. Boston: Colonial Society of Massachusetts, 1980.

Sechrest, Larry J. "Public Goods and Private Solutions in Maritime History." *Quarterly Journal of Austrian Economics* 7, no. 2 (Summer 2004).

Sidney Brooks Scholars. *Harwich Vessels, 1872–1900*. Harwich, MA: Harwich Historical Society, 1995.

Smith, Mary Lou. *Woods Hole Reflections*. Woods Hole, MA: Woods Hole Historical Collection, 1983.

Speck, Frank G. *Indian Notes and Monographs, No. 44. Territorial Subdivisions and Boundaries of the Wampanoag, Massachusetts, and Nauset Indians*. Edited by F.W. Hodge. Lancaster, PA: Lancaster Press, Inc., 1928.

Stackpole, Edouard A. *The Sea-Hunters: The Great Age of Whaling*. Philadelphia: J.B. Lippincott Company, 1953.

Swift, Charles F. *History of Old Yarmouth*. Edited by Charles A. Holbrooke Jr. Yarmouth Port, MA: Historical Society of Old Yarmouth, 1975.

Swift, E. Kent, Jr. "Swift Family Whaling." *Spritsail: A Journal of the History of Falmouth and Vicinity* 12 (1998): 20–25.

Thompson, Frederick L. *The Lightships of Cape Cod*. Portland, ME: Congress Square Press, 1983.

Thoreau, Henry David. *Cape Cod*. 1857. Reprinted Cape Cod, MA: Peninsula Press, 1997.

Travers, Milton A. *The Wampanoag Indian Federation: Indian Neighbors of the Pilgrims*. Boston: Christopher Publishing House, 1957.

Turner, Harry B. *The Story of the Island Steamers*. Nantucket, MA: Inquirer & Mirror, 1910.

Vickers, Daniel. "The First Whalemen of Nantucket." *William and Mary Quarterly* 40 (October 1983), 560–83.

Warbasse, James P., Jr. "From Sail to Steam to Diesel." *Spiritsail: A Journal of the History of Falmouth and Vicinity* 4, no. 2 (Summer 1990).

Watters, Gerry Geddes Buss. *Privateers, Pirates and Beyond: Memoirs of Lucy Lord Howes Hooper*. Dennis, MA: Dennis Historical Society, 2003.

Webber, Bernard C., WO USCG (Ret.). "The Captain Has the Last Word." Personal essay.

# BIBLIOGRAPHY

White, Robert Eldridge, Jr. *Eldridge Tide and Pilot Book 2008.*

Whynott, Douglas. *Giant Bluefin.* New York: HarperCollins, 1995.

*The William and Mary Quarterly*

Witzell, Susan Fletcher. *Walking Tour of Woods Hole Village.* Woods Hole, MA:
    self-published, 2008.

# INDEX

# ABOUT THE AUTHOR

Journalist and maritime author Theresa Mitchell Barbo is the founder and director of the annual Cape Cod Maritime History Symposium, now in partnership with the Cape Cod Museum of Natural History. Theresa is a noted lecturer on Cape Cod cultural heritage and maritime history before community organizations and at educational institutions. She holds BA and MA degrees from the University of Massachusetts Dartmouth and has studied executive integral leadership at the Mendoza College of Business at the University of Notre Dame.

Theresa lives in Yarmouth Port, Cape Cod, with her husband, Daniel, daughter Katherine and son Thomas. Her other books with The History Press are:

*The Cape Cod Murder of 1899*

*True Accounts of Yankee Ingenuity & Grit*

*Cape Cod Bay: A History of Salt & Sea*

*The Pendleton Disaster off Cape Cod:*
*The Greatest Small Boat Rescue in Coast Guard History*
second edition
With Captain W. Russell Webster, USCG (Ret.)
On Commandant's Recommended Reading List for Leadership

Visit us at
www.historypress.net